business *masterminds*

warren
BUFFETT

ROBERT HELLER

A Dorling Kindersley Book

DK www.dk.com

Dorling Kindersley
LONDON, NEW YORK, DELHI, JOHANNESBURG,
MUNICH, PARIS and SYDNEY

DK www.dk.com

Senior Editor Adèle Hayward
US Editor Gary Werner
Senior Art Editor Caroline Marklew
Project Art Editors Christine Lacey,
Laura Watson
DTP Designer Jason Little
Production Controller Elizabeth Cherry
Managing Editor Stephanie Jackson
Managing Art Editor Nigel Duffield

Produced for Dorling Kindersley by
Grant Laing Partnership 48 Brockwell
Park Gardens, London SE24 9BJ
Managing Editor Jane Laing
Project Editor Helen Ridge
Managing Art Editor Steve Wilson

Published in the United States by
Dorling Kindersley Publishing, Inc.
95 Madison Avenue
New York, New York 10016

First American Edition, 2000
2 4 6 8 10 9 7 5 3 1

Copyright © 2000
Dorling Kindersley Limited
Text copyright © 2000 Robert Heller

**Library of Congress Cataloging-in-
Publication Data**

Heller, Robert, 1932-
  Warren Buffett / Robert Heller.
    p. cm. – (Business masterminds)
  Includes bibliographical references and
index.
  ISBN 0-7894-5157-3 (acid-free paper)
    1. Buffett, Warren.
    2. Capitalists and financiers. I. Title.

HG172.B84 H45 2000
332.6'092–dc21   99-056840

Reproduced by Colourpath, London
Printed in Hong Kong by Wing King Tong

Author's Acknowledgments
The many sources for this book have been
acknowledged in the text, but I must now
express my great debt to everybody, above
all to the Mastermind himself. Nor would
the book exist but for the inspiration and
effort of the excellent Dorling Kindersley
team – to whom my warm thanks.

Packager's Acknowledgments
Grant Laing Partnership would like to
thank the following for their help and
participation:
Editorial Lee Stacy, Frank Ritter;
Design Sarah Williams;
Index Kay Ollerenshaw.

Publisher's Acknowledgments
Dorling Kindersley would like to thank the
following for their help and participation:
Editorial Josephine Bryan, Claire Ellerton,
Nicola Munro, Jane Simmonds;
Design Austin Barlow, Tracy Hambleton-
Miles, Laura Watson, Nigel Morris;
DTP Rob Campbell, Louise Waller;
Picture research Andy Sansom.

Contents

The greatest investor in the world

The multibillion dollar fortune of Warren Buffett is one of the wonders of the 20th-century world. He created this fortune entirely with investments, mostly through public companies available to any investor, and all of them channeled into one company: Berkshire Hathaway. And instead of following the fortunes of high-tech super-growth stars, Buffett bought massive stakes, mostly in ordinary shares, in long-established giants like American Express, Walt Disney, Coca-Cola, and Gillette.

Buffett's approach to investment is to search for fundamental values overlooked by the stock market. He has also followed an elementally simple rule: never invest unless you can find something worth buying.

The quintessential pragmatist, Buffett is interested only in realities and is free of any illusions, especially about himself. His influence on others' stock market behavior has, therefore, been limited, since markets are driven to a significant degree by fear, greed, and delusions. But his success has demonstrated that common sense and consistent rationality win the day even in irrational markets.

Robert Heller

Biography

Warren Buffett was born on August 30, 1930, in Omaha, Nebraska, where he lives and works to this day, earning for himself the affectionate title of "The Sage of Omaha." Though by no means a recluse, he believes that his Midwest location shields him from the frenzy of Wall Street. He came by his profession naturally enough: his father was an investment banker, who also served as a congressman in Washington, DC.

Applying Graham's ideas

Buffett learned the fundamentals of finance at the Wharton School of Finance, Pennsylvania, and then earned an economics degree from the University of Nebraska. Studying for his master's at Columbia Graduate Business School, Buffett came under the influence of Benjamin Graham. After working as an investment salesman for the family firm in Omaha from 1951 to 1954, Buffett moved to New York to work for Graham's investment company – Graham-Newman Corporation – as a securities analyst.

From 1956 to 1969, Buffett ran a private investment partnership in Omaha for well-to-do Nebraskans, including family and friends. He was very successful at applying Graham's ideas, searching for businesses whose intrinsic value – their real worth as going concerns – was greater than the stock price. The partnership was eventually liquidated to the great profit of the investors – and of Buffett. From 1970, he transcended that success, having acquired control in 1965 of Berkshire Hathaway, a textile company which, curiously, was one of his poorest investments (see p. 86).

Berkshire's meteoric rise

That hardly mattered, though, when Buffett began using Berkshire as a vehicle for other interests, including brilliant stock purchases. Over 34 years, the company achieved an astonishing 24.7 percent compound annual return for its shareholders. Buffett has been its chairman and chief executive officer from the start, working with a small staff and shunning almost all the trappings of great riches and executive eminence. But his wry personality, enormous success, and mounting billions in personal wealth have made him a legend — and the hero of his shareholders.

Any of them who bought shares in 1965 have seen spectacular results. Had they invested $10,000, it would now be worth $51 million. The chief beneficiaries from this miracle of investment have, of course, been Buffett and his family. His wife of 47 years, Susan, sits on the board, as do his daughter, also Susan, and Howard, one of his two sons. But neither these two nor Peter, the third child, play any management role. Buffett's right-hand man for many years was his vice-chairman, Charlie Munger. Regularly praised by Buffett, who gives his old friend a great share of the credit for Berkshire's success, Munger retired to the sidelines in 1999 at the age of 75.

Personal style

Some 15,000 shareholders flock to Omaha for Berkshire's annual general meeting. Throwing out the first ball for the local minor league baseball team has become one of Buffett's rituals for this weekend event. Investors can shop for jewelry at a company-owned store, vie for reservations at Gorat's, where Buffett likes to dine, and line up for the autographs of Buffett and Munger.

The personal touch and the homeyness are genuine; to an unusual extent, Buffett is what he seems. What the *Financial Times* once called his "wisecracks and folksy wisdom" accurately measure the man. It is characteristic of Buffett that virtually all of his wealth (an astounding $40 billion in May 1999, second only to that of Bill Gates) is invested in Berkshire. This, of course, gives him a tremendous spread, both in the share portfolio and in the company's wholly owned businesses. These range from Dairy Queen ice-cream parlors, bought for $590 million in 1998, to auto insurance and shoe manufacturing.

Being a contrarian investor

Berkshire also owns General Re, America's largest re-insurance company, which cost $22 billion in 1998, and all in stocks. Using stocks for investment purposes was something of a departure for Buffett, who had previously made a point of being a cash purchaser on almost every occasion. Such a preference is one of his several distinctive "contrarian" characteristics. As a contrarian, he has never followed the herd, and the herd has never followed him. In fact, his career has been built on a paradox. If everybody searched for and bought undervalued shares, their prices would rise rapidly until they were fully valued. Therefore, Buffett's unique success as an investor has depended on others not following his ideas.

In another paradox, the past success of his theories has now made it much harder for him to apply them. As the Berkshire wealth has boomed, so each new investment has had to be increasingly gigantic to make any impact on the whole. With a net worth of $57.4 billion in May 1999, his company faced a situation that Buffett described frankly:

"Our future rates of gain will fall far short of those achieved in the past. Berkshire's capital base is now simply too large to allow us to earn truly outsized returns. If you believe otherwise, you should consider a career in sales but avoid one in mathematics."

Because of the technical bookkeeping consequences of the General Re transaction, the gain in Berkshire's book value (see p. 52) in 1998 was 48.3 percent. Buffett has only bettered that annual increase once in his company's history. But the special contribution of General Re hid the fact that the stock market grew 10 times faster than Berkshire's $37.3 billion portfolio of shares. That was weighed down by three of Buffett's favorite holdings: Coca-Cola, Gillette, and Walt Disney, which all had a miserable 1998.

It appeared equally uncharacteristic of Buffett to invest heavily in copper in 1997, prompting memories of an earlier attempt to corner the market in metal, which ruined the super-rich Hunt brothers. No disaster attended Buffett's plunge into copper, but it was not a great success. In fact, Buffett has had some conspicuous failures, about which he talks more bluntly than anybody else. The worst episode was probably the scandal at Salomon Brothers Inc., the largest Wall Street investment bank; Buffett had to take the chair, and spend more time than he wanted away from Omaha, to save the bank and rescue his huge investment.

Accumulating businesses

But Buffett has not made a truly large investment in stocks since buying 4.3 percent of McDonald's in 1995. Since that purchase, Buffett has been busily converting Berkshire into a different kind of company. The purchase of General Re marked another stage in this process. In 1996,

Investing in brand power
Coca-Cola, an outstandingly successful investment, typifies the kind of company Buffett most favors: one focused on a single powerful brand that has a dominant share in an easily understood market.

74 percent of Berkshire's assets consisted of shares in other companies. Now stock market investments account for under a third of the Berkshire total worth. Buffett presides over $82 billion in wholly owned operating companies, which employ no less than 47,566 workers.

There is no pattern to this accumulation of businesses, except for the predominance taken by insurance, enhanced by the General Re purchase. Buffett's collection of insurers has sales of some $14 billion, and far outweighs the other sectors. The three largest of these, however, are still substantial: home furnishings bring in $793 million of sales, "flight services" produce over $850 million, and Scott Fetzer, a highly varied bundle of products, from vacuum cleaners to encyclopedias, has $1 billion in revenues.

Creating a conglomerate

Scott Fetzer is a typical example of a now unfashionable corporate breed – the "conglomerate," less flatteringly called a "ragbag." The noun fits Berkshire as a whole. Conglomerates as a corporate form are a long way removed from "value investing"; notoriously, most conglomerates have subtracted rather than added to the value of their subsidiaries. Buffett has always greatly favored investments in exactly the opposite kinds of company: those focused on powerful single brands, like Coca-Cola. But he is striving to build a company that will outlast him; a portfolio of stock market investments would not serve that purpose.

Whether a sprawling conglomerate will do so without its creator's magic touch is another, more difficult question. Few of the conglomerates built in their great era, the 1960s, survived their founders' departures. Buffett is in a new game. His rise to fabulous riches was built on the strong theoretical foundations learned from Benjamin Graham. But that theory governed picking stocks. Provided the buy was right, no further action was required, except collecting the dividends; the management decisions were taken by the company concerned, not by Buffett.

So far, Buffett has applied a similar approach to management, trusting the operating executives to deliver profits in suitable quantities. Now the old master needs to demonstrate that his management theories and practice, which have been applied very successfully so far, can be as effective as his investment ideas. That is a tall order.

1

Assessing the value of companies

How market values diverge from the "intrinsic value" of businesses ● **Three non-financial criteria for identifying an outstanding company** ● Four financial criteria that specifically relate to managerial excellence ● **Having the courage and conviction to put all your eggs in one basket** ● Following probability theory in the choice and timing of investments ● **Being indifferent to the day-to-day movement of stock prices** ● How to value a business and think about market prices

Buffett's ability to choose undervalued stocks is a living and amazingly successful denial of the academic theory that markets are "efficient," that is, the price of a security accurately sums up all the information available on the company and its stock. On the contrary, Buffett maintains (and, more significantly, has proved) that market values diverge, often markedly, from the "intrinsic value" of a business, which represents the real and lasting worth of its economic attributes.

Buffett looks for companies that have a history of stability as well as above-average performance. This seems a rational enough approach, and it has certainly been a successful one for him. Yet the theory appears to be founded on the fallacy that the past is a good guide to the future. Obviously, there can never be any certainty that either the stability or the superior performance will continue. But, in Buffett's view, it is simply more probable that a company with a good history will remain good than that a bad company, based on its historical record, will become good.

Focus investing

Buffett therefore proceeds with total confidence to implement an investment policy which, as explained by Robert G. Hagstrom, Jr., in *The Warren Buffett Portfolio* (1999), looks like simplicity itself: "Choose a few stocks that are likely to produce above-average returns over the long haul, concentrate the bulk of your investments in those stocks, and have the fortitude to hold steady during any short-term market gyrations."

This policy of what is termed "focus investing" belongs to neither of the two warring schools of thought that actually dominate modern stock market investment. Most investment funds, from pensions to mutual funds, are actively run by their managers, whose employment, rewards, and reputations rest on their ability to pick shares that out-perform the market. They typically buy a great number of stocks in order to "spread the risks."

The fund managers, in effect, use a shotgun rather than a rifle – although they claim to be sharpshooters, of course. As Buffett has often pointed out, the more stocks they buy, the more likely they are, at best, only to match the performance of the market as a whole. That being so, argue proponents of the second school of thought, why not simply invest in the whole market? Instead of picking individual stocks, index funds "track" a popular stock market index. The problem here, however, is that, by definition, it is impossible to "outperform" the market.

Meeting non-financial criteria

Buffett recommends index funds for the uninformed investor; but that choice only makes sense for those who truly believe that stock market performance is entirely random and not susceptible to human reasoning. That is not Buffett's view. He believes that rationality rules in all matters, including, first, how you identify an outstanding company. He applies three non-financial criteria:

- It is simple and understandable.
- It has a consistent operating history.
- It has favorable long-term prospects.

The first criterion bars Buffett from high-technology, gee-whiz investment and therefore from participating in phenomenal growth sagas such as that of Microsoft, the creation of his friend Bill Gates. The argument is that if you cannot understand the business, you cannot make a rational judgment of its investment value. Given that so many other opportunities exist, why go into situations where one arm is tied behind your back?

The "consistent operating history" speaks for itself; Buffett no more wants volatile management than volatile technology. But the next insistence, on "favorable long-term prospects," ventures into futurology. He is again extrapolating the past into the future. When investing in Coca-Cola, for example, he is not betting on some

The billionaire buddies
Warren Buffett and Bill Gates, the two richest men in America, are close personal friends. Despite that, Buffett will not buy Microsoft shares because he only invests where he understands the technology.

marvelous new drink yet to be born. He is assuming that existing markets for existing beverages will continue to expand steadily, that further new markets will generate further rapid growth, that Coca-Cola's marketing skills will still sustain its share, and that its financial management will optimize profitability.

Any of these propositions might be falsified by events, as actually happened to Coca-Cola from 1998 to 1999. But once again Buffett is betting on the probabilities and on the "long term." Over several years, he reckons, the chances are that reverses will be more than corrected. The proviso is that the company must enjoy a management that follows three requirements: it must be rational; it must be candid with shareholders; and it must resist the "institutional imperative," that is, the irrational tendency of corporate leaders to imitate other managements' practices and policies, irrespective of their suitability or sense.

Meeting financial criteria

Naturally, Buffett expects financial benefits to flow from this good managerial behavior. His financial criteria, though, are not those used by most investment analysts. Because excellent profits are the result of good management, Buffett watches indicators that specifically relate to managerial excellence. He looks at:

- Return on equity (not earnings per share)
- "Owner earnings" (the share of profits that belongs to investors)
- Profit margins (which must be high)
- Return on reinvested profits (which must create at least $1 of market value for every dollar reinvested)

The majority of public companies will fail on at least one of Buffett's three non-financial and four financial criteria, thus narrowing his field of choice substantially. If a company has passed muster on all these counts, Buffett can proceed to the two crucial issues: First, what is the business truly worth, that is, what is its "intrinsic value"? And, second, is the market value significantly lower than that true worth? Of course, by insisting that the chosen investment should be within your area of personal knowledge, Buffett narrows the field still further.

Putting your eggs in one basket

This insistence on a restricted area of investment paves the way toward investing in only five to ten securities, as Buffett recommends. His argument is that the risk actually increases when investments are spread too thinly. Instead, he commands: "Put all your eggs in one basket – and watch that basket."

Buffett can quote substantial authority for this line of reasoning, not only Philip Fisher, the famous American investment adviser who put his eggs in very few baskets, but also the great Cambridge economist John Maynard Keynes. In 1934, Keynes wrote: "One's knowledge and experience are definitely limited and there are seldom more than two or three enterprises at any given time in which I personally feel myself entitled to put *full* confidence."

The logic behind Keynes's argument and Buffett's practice is unassailable. However, it is incomplete. The investor is being asked to put total faith in his or her own judgment, even though the three, or five, or 10, or 15 stocks chosen are unlikely to be the very best choices available. Each decision to buy excludes other investments that may perform better. The diversified investors prefer a wider choice to reduce dependence on their judgment and thus reduce the risk of being wrong. Accepting that risk is not so much a matter of logic as of courage, Buffett is very clear on this vital point: "With each investment you make, you should have the courage and the conviction to place at least 10 percent of your net worth in that stock."

Judging the probabilities

If you trust your own judgment, the courage and the conviction are rational. Yet the stock market is irrational. So, how can this apparent contradiction be resolved? Here mathematics enters the picture. To Buffett, investment is a matter of judging the "probabilities." Probability theory is a very important and respectable branch of mathematics, and it is essential to Buffett's theory of investment: "Take the probability of loss times the amount of possible loss from the probability of gain times the amount of possible gain. That is what we're trying to do. It's imperfect, but that's what it is all about."

Probabilities are basic to the art of arbitrage, at which Buffett is a master. The principle of arbitrage is to estimate the probable result if a given event occurs, for example,

"Our goal is to find an outstanding business at a sensible price, not a mediocre business at a bargain price. Charlie and I have found making silk purses out of silk is the best that we can do; with sows' ears we fail."
The Essays of Warren Buffett

if an announced takeover bid succeeds. If it looks as though the stock in the company concerned can be bought for a value lower than the probable outcome, Buffett becomes interested. To illustrate the point, one year Berkshire made a very easy $64 million after the announcement of a takeover bid by Kohlberg Kravis & Roberts (KKR), the investment specialists, for the food and tobacco giant RJR Nabisco.

Buffett's approach to arbitrage is essentially the same as his investment strategy. In both cases, he buys into situations where the probability is that the stocks are undervalued and that this undervaluation will be corrected. The difference is time-scale; the arbitrage position will be closed out as soon as possible, while the investment will be kept "indefinitely so long as we expect the business to increase in intrinsic value at a satisfactory rate." That answers the question about how long Buffett believes a stock should be held: possibly forever.

Calculating value

Buffett makes the crucial point that he and Munger have invested "as business analysts – not as market analysts, not as macroeconomic analysts, and not even as security analysts." The basic task is calculating value, for instance, that of the Washington Post Company in mid-1973. Buffett says that the general estimate of WPC's "intrinsic business value" would have been $400–500 million, even though it was valued on the stock market at only $100 million. So Buffett bought and, following another of his principles, bought big. A quarter of a century later, Berkshire still holds the stock, which continues to satisfy Buffett's requirements for keeping shares:

- The prospective return on equity capital of the underlying business is satisfactory.
- Management is competent and honest.
- The market does not overvalue the business.

The third requirement raises a difficulty. Buffett says flatly that sometimes "the market may judge a business to be more valuable than the underlying facts would indicate it is. In such a case, we will sell our holdings." Yet his practice and his words suggest that he is a very reluctant seller. He refers to "primary holdings" (including WPC) that "we expect to keep permanently." As he explains: "Even if these securities were to appear significantly overpriced, we would not anticipate selling them, just as we would not sell See's [the candy business] or *Buffalo Evening News* if someone were to offer us a price far above what we believe those businesses are worth."

This statement demonstrates that Buffett makes no distinction between two investment activities: buying part of a company through the stock market and buying all of a company by private treaty. On the same analogy, he is indifferent to the stock market behavior of the stocks he purchases: "We don't need a daily quote on our 100 percent position in See's... to validate our well-being. Why, then, should we need a quote on our 7 percent interest in Coke?"

"Consciously paying more for a stock than its calculated value... should be labeled speculation (which is neither illegal, immoral, nor – in our view – financially fattening)."
The Essays of Warren Buffett

Irresistible business strength

The value of Buffett's primary holdings, using his own approach, lies not in the stock market quotation but in the calculable, irresistible business strength of companies like those he calls "The Inevitables":

> "Is it really so difficult to conclude that Coca-Cola and Gillette possess far less business risk over the long term than, say, any computer company or retailer? Worldwide, Coke sells about 44 percent of all soft

A base in Nebraska
Buffett believes that working from his home town, Omaha, insulates him from the frenetic activity of the Wall Street financial houses, whose sophisticated knowledge, he says, is not needed by investors.

drinks, and Gillette has more than a 60 percent share (in value) of the blade market. Leaving aside chewing gum, in which Wrigley is dominant, I know of no other significant businesses in which the leading company has long enjoyed such global power."

Buffett adds that "both Coke and Gillette have actually increased their worldwide shares of market in recent years." He argues correctly that these companies, through "the might of their brand names, the attributes of their products, and the strength of their distribution systems," have "an enormous competitive advantage."

But how reliable is the consequent "protective moat around their economic castles"? The rational answer is that no company is an "Inevitable." Emotionally, though, Buffett feels deeply attached to those investments that have served him so well. It is unlike the rational Buffett to make irrational judgments about inevitability. Nevertheless, it is as difficult to find any chinks in Buffett's investment armor as it is to fault the success of his strategies. Their strength lies in their simplicity.

Unnecessary knowledge

Sophisticated knowledge of markets and finance, he says, is not vital, or even necessary: "You may, in fact, be better off knowing nothing" about "efficient market theory," or modern portfolio theory, option pricing, or emerging markets. Buffett observes caustically that this "of course, is not the prevailing view at most business schools, whose finance curriculum tends to be dominated by such subjects." In Buffett's view, investment students need only two courses ("well-taught," naturally): how to value a business and how to think about market prices.

These business courses would be short ones, too, judging by Buffett's summary of what the goal for an investor should be: "to purchase, at a rational price, a part interest in an easily understandable business whose earnings are virtually certain to go intrinsically higher five, 10, and 20 years from now." There are three important missing pieces from this formula, however: what is a "rational" price?; how certain is "virtually certain"?; and what is the meaning of "intrinsically higher" earnings?

Obviously, an "over-priced" purchase — one made at an irrational price exceeding the intrinsic business value — will not deliver the next leg of Buffett's strategic intent. He assumes that if a company's intrinsic earnings (those from its underlying business) grow materially, say, by 20 percent a year, the stock price will rise correspondingly. Pay too much at the outset and the likelihood of future advances in earnings will be seriously diminished.

Time may help to correct your error, provided you let it. Buffett says firmly that "if you aren't willing to own a stock for 10 years, don't even think about owning it for 10 minutes. Put together a portfolio of companies whose aggregate earnings march upward over the years, and so also will the portfolio's market value." Buffett adds in his best self-deprecating manner that "lethargy bordering on sloth remains the cornerstone of our investment style." In one year, for instance, Berkshire neither bought nor sold a share in five of its six major holdings. That is the final building block of his investment strategy. If you can't find anything worth buying, don't.

The strategy is a minority one. Many investors, especially professionals, not only buy many stocks but change them often, thus generating, as Buffett observes, nothing except commissions for stockbrokers. However, he rejects the label (which he is often given) of "contrarian," one who goes against the crowd, even though that, very obviously, is what he does. He observes that adopting a contrarian approach for its own sake is "just as foolish as a follow-the-crowd strategy." Rather, Buffett approvingly quotes Bertrand Russell: "Most men would rather die than think. Many do." If thinking long and hard before investing makes Buffett a contrarian, that is fine by him.

Ideas into action

- Look for companies with a history of stability and above-average performance.

- Only make investments that are within your own area of knowledge.

- Put all your eggs in one basket – and proceed to watch that basket.

- Make your investments as a business analyst, not as a security analyst.

- Regard the buying of a stock as if you were buying the whole company.

- Do without a sophisticated knowledge of markets and finance.

- Always be willing to own a stock for a minimum of 10 years.

Sitting at the feet of the master

Warren Buffett was a student at the University of Nebraska when he discovered a book that, more than anything else, launched his career as a radical investment thinker and a sensationally successful practitioner.

The book was *The Intelligent Investor* by Benjamin Graham (right), who taught at Columbia Graduate Business School. Enormously impressed by Graham's writings, Buffett went to graduate school at Columbia specifically to sit at the master's feet.

His own mathematical talents made him highly responsive to Graham's central teaching: that the "intrinsic value" of a company could be worked out quite accurately, and that its stock should only be purchased when its price was below the calculated value. The degree of that undervaluation he termed the "margin of safety." Graham also taught Buffett the right "mental attitude" toward market fluctuations. That mind-set was built around "a remarkably accommodating fellow named Mr. Market who... appears daily and names a price at which he will either buy your interest [in a private business] or sell you his." Mr. Market has "incurable emotional problems" that cause

his named prices to fluctuate wildly between optimism and pessimism. But you are not interested in anything but that price and whether it interests you. Mr. Market is there to serve you, not to guide you. It is his wallet, not his wisdom, that concerns you.

Theory into practice

Buffett bore Graham's advice in mind when he worked for his father's stockbroking company, starting in 1952. He kept up the relationship with Graham, and after two years accepted his invitation to join the Graham-Newman Corporation in New York. The firm specialized in arbitrage – taking advantage of the differences in price between quotations for securities and what they were worth if, for example, an announced takeover deal went through.

While working for Graham-Newman, Buffett calculated that its earnings from arbitrage averaged 20 percent annually over the whole period from 1926 to 1956 – which bridged the Great

"The key to successful investing was the purchase of shares in good businesses when market prices were at a large discount from underlying business values." *The Essays of Warren Buffett*

Crash. This analysis of winning returns, not from inside information but from "highly publicized" events, convinced Buffett that Grahamite theories worked   that "Mr. Market" often got it wrong.

Having mastered and proved Graham's theories, Buffett was ready to apply them in practice. Using $100 of his own money, the 25-year-old Buffett set up an investment partnership in Omaha. The seven partners were personal friends who trusted Buffett to handle their investments, and contributed $100,000 between them. With $100,100 thus at his disposal, Buffett's target was high: to beat the market, as measured by the Dow Jones Industrial Average, by 10 points a year. By the time Buffett closed the partnership in 1969, he had easily beaten the target, topping the Dow by 22 points – with an average annual return of 30.4 percent. Graham's "margin of safety" had worked for the disciple even more wonderfully than the master would have expected.

Investing in stocks

Buffett's teachings on investment sound deceptively simple. But there is no deception. They truly are simple. Do not allow investment advisers to persuade you that investment is a complex matter needing great expertise. Instead, learn how to assess the fundamental and financial values of a business yourself, and invest according to your convictions.

Ignoring convention

To invest well you must be prepared to go against the prevailing wisdom and ignore conventional investment guidelines. So:

- Do not put your eggs in many baskets.
- Do not place small amounts in each basket.
- Do not switch holdings frequently.
- Do not avoid holding cash.
- Do not rely on outside analysis.
- Do not often act on a hunch.
- Do not follow the crowd.
- Do not watch the market intently.
- Have fixed investment principles.

Contrarian principles

The conventional approach, Buffett believes, makes it difficult to beat the market and easy to do worse. Increase your chances of finding winning stocks by adhering to Buffett's contrarian principles.

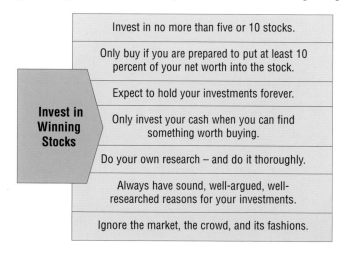

Invest in Winning Stocks

Invest in no more than five or 10 stocks.

Only buy if you are prepared to put at least 10 percent of your net worth into the stock.

Expect to hold your investments forever.

Only invest your cash when you can find something worth buying.

Do your own research – and do it thoroughly.

Always have sound, well-argued, well-researched reasons for your investments.

Ignore the market, the crowd, and its fashions.

1 Assessing value

All investors hope to find a bargain. Conventional investors measure value by looking at factors relating to the market price. Buffett urges you to look only at the fundamental worth of the business.

Investigating the business

Valuing a business involves assessing the quality of its customer franchise and management, about which market rating tells nothing.

Valuing a Business
Make sure you understand the business thoroughly.
Ask whether the business has consistently increased sales and operating profits over time.
Determine if it is reasonable to expect this consistent performance to continue into the distant future.

Are you able to rate management's quality? You have a better chance of judging how well a business is run, and its likely future performance, if you focus on firms that are within your personal knowledge – including any that you know well through direct personal contact. Do all the research you can:

- Buy a few shares in any business that interests you and attend the annual general meeting to get a look at the management.
- Read all you can about the business, especially its management, in press clippings, on the Internet, in its annual reports, etc.
- If possible, use its products and services, rate them against competitive products and services, inspect its premises, and test its responsiveness to customers.

Assessing financial value

When you are as confident as possible that the business you have studied has good long-term prospects, you move on to the next stage. How does your assessment translate into financial value? And how does that valuation compare with the market price? Remember that unless the latter is markedly below your judgment of the true, or intrinsic, value, you should not buy.

2 Measuring the financials

Before investing in a business that you judge to have favorable prospects, you must assess whether its true, or intrinsic, value promises you a large enough return on your capital in the longer term. To be sure of your assessment, take Buffett's advice and thoroughly investigate the financial standing of the business before making any decision to buy.

Calculating intrinsic value

Your self-confidence should be increased by Buffett's insistence that sophisticated financial knowledge is not required. The definition of intrinsic value does rest on a mathematical concept – and there are technicalities involved. Putting them on one side, the basic proposition is simple: compare your proposed stock-market investment, which carries an element of risk, with a risk-free alternative. The argument is as follows:

- A top-rated government bond is as near to a risk-free investment as you will ever find.
- If the annual interest is 9 percent, its return over 100 years is 900 percent of a purchase price of 100.
- Unless the shares in an organization can beat this return, they are plainly not worth buying.

So Buffett looks for companies where the net cash coming into the business can be expected to grow, for all intents and purposes forever, at a percentage appreciably above the interest on long-term government bonds. The difference between these two future streams of money determines the present-day "intrinsic value" of the shares and, therefore, whether they are worth buying.

Predicting future profits

Buffett always does these calculations before investing. You will see that they rest on prediction, which is always a risky business. But you must also turn your favorable view of the company's prospects into hard numbers. What are you actually hoping for, and how realistic is that hope? Buffett's concept carries a powerful lesson you dare not ignore:

Always do your math before investing.

Finding the figures

Some of the figures that you need to assess a company's financial prospects must be dug out of the published accounts. Buffett seeks the answers to four critical questions:

Four Key Financial Questions
1 What percentage is the company earning on the shareholders' capital (or equity)?
2 How much are the earnings that belong to the shareholders?
3 What are the profit margins?
4 Does the company create at least $1 of market value for every $1 of shareholder funds that it keeps in the business?

Earnings to equity ratio

The first question is the easiest to answer; many companies publish the figure. Equity is the company's capital minus its long-term debt. Divide that into the profits after tax to find the percentage return. This must be significantly higher than the return on long-term bonds. As a rule-of-thumb, a company with a 15-percent return on equity can be expected to grow its value by 15 percent per annum.

Shareholder earnings

Working out "owner-earnings" means adding to after-tax profits the funds set aside for financial reasons – above all, depreciation. While the company must allow for the eventual replacement of its plant and equipment, etc., the cash is not being spent now. Adding back depreciation, plus the company's share of any profits from interests in other companies, gives you a truer picture of its earning power.

Profit margins

To answer the third question, you need to measure the strength of the company's "franchise" (its customer base) and its business model (in other words, the relationship between its costs and its prices). Look at operating profits as a percentage of sales. Analyze the results carefully; too low a figure (under 5 percent) is a discouraging sign, while too high a figure (over 20 percent) could be unsustainable.

Market value

The fourth question is absolutely vital to your overall assessment of the fundamental value of the business. Add back the "retained" profits that were not paid out in tax and dividends over, say, three years. Compare the company's market value at the start of the period with that at the end. Does the difference add up to more than the retained profits? That is the only way in which management can demonstrate its ability to use shareholders' money wisely and well.

Exercising caution

You are of necessity relying on published accounts. Buffett warns that these often contain misleading figures, sometimes deliberately so. Look carefully at the cashflow. If it is heading down when the profit is going up, be very wary. Remember that a company's accounts will nearly always juggle profits upward rather than downward. That being the case, discouraging answers to the four key questions are even more worrying than they seem at first sight.

Buying below market value

There is another rule-of-thumb that will help you to evaluate a business. In the case of Mrs. Blumkin and the Nebraska Furniture Mart (see p. 48), Buffett bought a successful business with capable management for substantially less than the value of its annual sales. Unless there is a sinister explanation, a low ratio of market value to sales is an encouraging sign.

Misleading figures

You cannot bank the profits shown in the accounts. You can only bank the cash coming in. If that is less than the cash going out, bankruptcy may result.

Rolls-Royce, Britain's most famous company, announced decent profits year after year, despite heavy spending on aero-engine research and development. The spending, however, was not charged in the accounts against profits, but added to them as "the value of R&D recoverable from sales resulting from existing orders." The company still had to find the cash to pay for all the R&D. Re-examination of the accounts showed that the cashflow was negative, and Rolls-Royce could only pay the dividend by raising money from the shareholders! Eventually, the company ran out of cash and just went bankrupt.

3 Managing the investment

If your research indicates that the shares are available below their intrinsic value, you have a "margin of safety." You can make the investment. Now you have to manage it successfully.

Holding stocks

Buffett has no use for investment management in the usual sense: the active buying and selling of stocks across a large number of holdings on a day-to-day basis. Rather, he points out the advantages of investing so wisely that you never have to sell a share.

The Advantages of Not Selling
No dealing costs
No taxation on your capital gains
The magic of compound interest

The third advantage is the most important in the argument for keeping stocks long-term. In *The Warren Buffett Portfolio*, Robert G. Hagstrom illustrates these advantages by setting out two outcomes from a brilliant $1,000 investment that doubles in value every year.

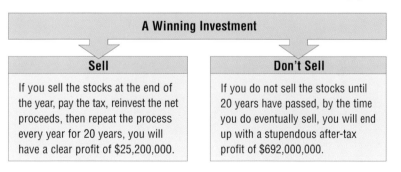

A Winning Investment	
Sell	**Don't Sell**
If you sell the stocks at the end of the year, pay the tax, reinvest the net proceeds, then repeat the process every year for 20 years, you will have a clear profit of $25,200,000.	If you do not sell the stocks until 20 years have passed, by the time you do eventually sell, you will end up with a stupendous after-tax profit of $692,000,000.

This, of course, is a fairy-tale exercise. But the principle is absolutely real. Never forget it. Remember "Mr. Market," who is always ready to buy or sell. You are only interested in him when he wants to sell to you at well below market value or to buy well above it. In the first case, you buy. In the second, you seriously consider taking your profit.

2

Making acquisitions pay

Why, in most acquisitions, it is better to be the target ● **The importance of being active, interested, but never in a hurry** ● Understanding that a managerial kiss will not turn a toadlike business into a princely one ● **How issuing stocks in acquisitions amounts to a partial sale** ● Ensuring that the opportunity's value matches or surpasses any alternative ● **Paying careful attention to the post-acquisition management of the buy** ● Concentrating on two tasks: capital allocation and the top appointment

Most mergers and acquisitions take place at a premium above the current stock market price. To Buffett, this is seldom justifiable. Sometimes, especially able managers buy apparently fully valued businesses whose greater, unrecognized worth they proceed to unlock. But Buffett does not play this game; he is interested in one factor alone: the intrinsic value of a company, not its stock market value.

He accepts that mergers are often motivated by sound strategic consideration, and that "there truly are synergies in a great many mergers." But the existence and exploitation of these synergies — the savings and other benefits from combining the two forces — are not the sole driving force. Managers are activated more by the desire to enhance the size of their corporation or by the excitement of acquisition. That is why Buffett is certain that mergers will continue:

"You don't get to be the CEO of a big company by being a milquetoast. You are not devoid of animal spirits. And it gets contagious. I've been a director of 19 different public companies over the years, and I can tell you that the conversation turns to acquisitions and mergers much more when the competitors of the particular company are engaging in those."

The animal spirits and the bandwagon effect are stronger when stock markets are generally buoyant, which "tends to encourage mergers, because everybody's currency [their stocks] is more useful in those circumstances." But Buffett is in no doubt that the advantage usually lies with the seller: "In most acquisitions, it's better to be the target than the acquirer. The acquirer pays for the fact that he gets to haul back to his cave the carcass of the conquered animal." That payment helps to make Buffett "suspicious of people who just keep acquiring almost by the week."

Hunting for acquisitions

Buffett prefers to see organic growth, and notes that outstanding companies – "a Microsoft or an Intel or a Wal Mart," for example – have relied overwhelmingly on internal expansion, as opposed to companies that are "on a real acquisition binge." Frequently, "they feel they're using funny money, and it has certain aspects of a chain-letter game." The "funny money" is often followed by funny accounting, which Buffett would like to see countered by instituting "a period where merged companies just run by themselves after a deal" without any financial changes.

This has always been Berkshire Hathaway's approach to its own purchases, of which there have been many. In fact, Buffett regards acquisition as "the most exhilarating" of all the activities in which he and Charlie Munger have participated. They seek only businesses that have "excellent economic characteristics and a management that we like, trust, and admire." Buffett is constantly on the hunt, but never "acquisition-hungry," rather adopting "the same attitude one might find appropriate in looking for a spouse. It pays to be active, interested, and open-minded, but it does not pay to be in a hurry."

Characteristically, this view is based on experience and observation, and not on theory. Buffett has "observed that many acquisition-hungry managers were apparently mesmerized by their childhood reading of the story about the frog-kissing princess [whose kiss turned the frog into a handsome prince]":

> "Remembering her success, they pay dearly for the right to kiss corporate toads, expecting wondrous transfigurations. Initially, disappointing results only deepen their desire to round up new toads... Ultimately, even the most optimistic manager must

face reality. Standing knee-deep in unresponsive toads, he then announces an enormous 'restructuring' charge... the CEO receives the education but the stockholders pay the tuition."

Good businesses at fair prices

Buffett has, characteristically, made his own mistakes in buying businesses and learned from them. He recalls his early days as a manager: "I, too, dated a few toads. They were cheap dates... but my results matched those of acquirers who courted higher-priced toads. I kissed and they croaked." His conclusion "after several failures of this type" was to follow the advice of a golf pro: "Practice doesn't make perfect; practice makes permanent." So, Buffett revised his strategy "and tried to buy good businesses at fair prices rather than fair businesses at good prices."

To put this another way, Buffett aims his acquisition strategy at maximizing real economic benefits. His positive thoughts on how you achieve this end, however, are built on avoiding the negative steps taken by other managements. Many of the latter are mesmerized by size for its own sake and deceived into believing that "their managerial kiss will do wonders for the profitability of Company T(arget)." Buffett acknowledges that some "managerial superstars" have the ability to turn toads into princes, but remarks that both changeable toads and kissing superstars are rarities.

On the other hand, Buffett recounts that: "We have done well with a couple of princes – but they were princes when purchased. At least our kisses didn't turn them into toads. And, finally, we have occasionally been quite successful in purchasing fractional interests in easily identifiable princes at toadlike prices."

Growing organically
Buffett cites Wal-Mart as an example of an outstanding company that has relied on internal expansion for growth, unlike many businesses that embark on doomed acquisition binges.

Full business value

Buffett has strong views on the "currency" that should be used in acquisitions: either stocks or cash. His "simple basic rule" is that "we will not issue shares unless we receive as much intrinsic business value as we give." He notes that "such a ploy might seem axiomatic," as anything else prompts the obvious question, "Why... would anyone issue dollar bills in exchange for fifty-cent pieces?" The

CEO, Buffett allows, may initially prefer to use cash or debt. But his "cravings" may "outpace cash and credit resources."

The CEO's problem arises because the purchased company will usually sell for its "full business value." The purchaser could itself receive this full value if it sold out completely: "But when the buyer makes a partial sale of itself — *and that is what the issuance of stocks to make an acquisition amounts to* — it can customarily get no higher value set on its shares than the market chooses to grant it." That value, so Buffett's investment philosophy argues, is often below intrinsic value. The acquirer is paying more in value than is being received.

"Under such circumstances," Buffett observes, "a marvelous business purchased at a fair sales price becomes a terrible buy." He has no difficulty in demolishing the three rationalizations used by the managements who place themselves in this fix. The arguments are:

- *The company we're buying is going to be worth a lot more in the future.*
  BUT the value of the buyer will also presumably increase, so the imbalance in price will remain.
- *We have to grow.*
  BUT who is the "we" who have to grow? "For present shareholders, the reality is that all existing businesses shrink when shares are issued." That is, the shareholders' interest in the "old" businesses is automatically reduced.
- *Our stock is undervalued and we've minimized its use in this deal — but we need to give the selling shareholder 51 percent in stock and 49 percent in cash so that certain of those shareholders can get the tax-free exchange they want.*
  BUT the purchaser should put the interests of his own shareholders first.

Destruction of value

Buffett dismisses the irrational policies that result from such management rationalizations in a phrase that is his anathema: "destruction of value." A true business-value-for-business-value merger (Buffett's own speciality) is the exception. "It's not that acquirers wish to avoid such deals; it's just that they are very hard to do," he says. Exceptions also arise when the acquirer's stock is selling above its intrinsic value. In these cases, "the shareholders of the acquired company receive an inflated currency (frequently pumped up by dubious accounting and promotional techniques)."

Buffett was writing long before the age of the Internet and its stratospheric stock market valuations. The securities concerned, however, have been used mainly to buy other hype-inflated stock. In that case, the actual values being exchanged may be the same, although nobody can possibly know that for a fact. But Buffett's major conclusion still stands. If the issue of shares dilutes the value of the acquirer's equity, the initial destruction of shareholders' wealth will be compounded by a relative decline in the acquirer's share price. He points out: "Other things being equal, the highest stock market prices relative to intrinsic business value are given to companies whose managers have demonstrated their unwillingness to issue shares at any time on terms unfavorable to the owners of the business."

"Most major acquisitions... are a bonanza for the shareholders of the acquiree... But, alas, they usually reduce the wealth of the acquirer's shareholders...."
The Essays of Warren Buffett

It is abundantly clear that Buffett and Munger are extremely skeptical about acquisitions: "We believe most deals do damage to the shareholders of the acquiring company." This raises a question that Buffett himself poses. All of Berkshire's wholly owned companies, of course, have been acquired, so how have the two men avoided the traps? The first answer is that they never look at earnings

Inflated Internet stock
Many runaway Internet stock market stars are using their inflated stocks as cheap currency to purchase other hype-inflated companies whose intrinsic business value is impossibly difficult to determine.

projections prepared by sellers: "[We] never give them a glance, but instead keep in mind the story of the man with an ailing horse. Visiting the vet, he said: 'Can you help me? Sometimes my horse walks just fine and sometimes he limps.' The vet's reply was pointed: 'No problem – when he's walking fine, sell him.'"

Deciding to buy

Buffett and Munger do not have a strategic plan when it comes to making acquisitions: "We feel no need to proceed in an ordained direction (a course leading almost invariably to silly purchase prices)." They simply compare any proposed buy with the dozens of other opportunities available, including "the purchases of small pieces of the best businesses in the world via the stock market." They only proceed when they are satisfied that the acquisition opportunity matches or surpasses the value of any alternative. That means the buys will:

- Be large purchases (unless after-tax earnings are very large, Buffett will not consider the buy)
- Have demonstrated consistent earning power ("future projections are of little interest to us, nor are 'turnaround' situations")
- Be businesses earning good returns on equity while employing little or no debt
- Have management in place ("we can't supply it")
- Be simple businesses ("if there's lots of technology, we won't understand it")
- Have an offer price ("we don't want to waste our time or that of the seller by talking, even preliminarily, about a transaction when price is unknown")

But Buffett is, above all, not a financial wheeler-dealer. Since he buys for the long term, expecting to hold his purchases for ever, Berkshire is obliged to pay careful attention to an issue that seldom engages corporate acquirers – that is, how to manage the buy after acquisition, or rather, in Berkshire's case, how to not manage them.

Admitting to error

Buffett departed from his own expectation of holding stocks forever when he sold McDonald's in 1998, after only three years – and just before a large rise: "My decision to sell was a very big mistake."

Post-acquisition autonomy

Buffett's objective after the purchase is to secure the best possible performance from the acquired company. Presumably, other buyers share the same aim, but the great majority seek to reach that objective by intervention in the affairs of the new company. Buffett does not, and this allows him to claim that:

> "Berkshire offers something special. Our managers operate with extraordinary autonomy. Additionally, our ownership structure enables sellers to know that when I say we are buying to keep, the promise means something. For our part, we like dealing with owners who care what happens to their companies and people. A buyer is likely to find fewer unpleasant surprises dealing with that type of seller."

This preferred type of seller will "care about placing the companies in a corporate home that will both endure and provide pleasant, productive working conditions for the managers." That is also greatly in Buffett's interest. What advantage can there be in a transient purchase whose management, after acquisition, suffers unpleasant and counterproductive treatment?

Of all the various aspects of Buffett's acquisition theory, this emphasis on the performance and contentment of the acquired management is the simplest and hardest to fault. You may be able to argue (rightly or wrongly) that a "strategic" acquisition is justified, despite its excessive price, because it extends the reach of the corporation or prevents a competitor from seizing a real advantage. But it is impossible to argue a case for post-acquisition management that does not encourage and enable the acquired managers to give of their best in conditions of security and stability.

Avoiding intervention

Buffett emphasizes that an owner-manager sells the business "only once — frequently in an emotionally charged atmosphere with a multitude of pressures coming from different directions." As he says, "mistakes made in the once-in-a-lifetime sale of a business are not reversible." Post-acquisition management, he argues, is so often ineffective for two reasons:

- If the buyer is in much the same business, it "will usually have managers who feel they know how to run your business operations and, sooner or later, will want to apply some hands-on 'help'."
- The buyer's management "will have their own way of doing things and, even though your business record undoubtedly will be far better than theirs, human nature will at some point cause them to believe that their methods of operating are superior."

Berkshire is saved from the second temptation, partly because it is less likely to operate in the same business, even more because "we don't have, and don't expect to have, operating people in our parent organization." This has a simple yet powerful consequence: "When we buy a business, the sellers go on running it just as they did before the sale; we adapt to their methods rather than *vice versa*."

This leaves Buffett to concentrate on just two tasks: allocating capital and selecting and "compensating the top man." Other personnel decisions, operating strategies, etc., are that top man's bailiwick. "Some Berkshire managers talk over some of their decisions with me; some don't. It depends on their personalities and, to an extent, upon their own personal relationship with me."

Buffett does, however, believe in imposing one condition when buying a family business: he leaves 20 percent of the stocks in the hands of the operating members of the family. "Very simply, we would not want to buy unless we felt key members of present management would stay on as our partners. Contracts cannot guarantee your continued interest; we would simply rely on your word." The language, as always with Buffett, is crystal-clear and homespun. But it goes to the heart of acquisition success – and failure.

Ideas into action

- Look for organic growth first before you consider acquisitions.

- Be prepared to wait until a satisfactory deal comes along.

- Buy good businesses at fair prices, not fair businesses at good prices.

- Seek only a true exchange of business value for business value.

- Never look at earnings projections that have been prepared by sellers.

- Don't spend time on discussion unless a price is already known.

- Give management an ownership interest in the success of the business.

Buying and retaining Mrs. Blumkin

Buffett has, from the early days, preferred buying 100 percent of businesses to investing in only part of their equity. He loves the personal involvement with these businesses and their managements.

Their attractions are exemplified in an acquisition made in 1983: Nebraska Furniture Mart. As a local, Buffett knew this discount business well. It had been created and developed by Mrs. Rose Blumkin, who started with only $500. By the time Buffett took an interest, sales were $100 million-plus, generated from one 200,000 sq-ft store. Buffett found that Nebraska Furniture Mart outperformed any other US home furnishings store, and that the store's sales of furniture, carpets, and appliances exceeded those of all competitors in Omaha (right) put together.

The Blumkins easily passed a favorite Buffett test: "One question I always ask myself in appraising a business is how I would like, assuming I had ample capital and skilled personnel, to compete with it. I'd rather wrestle grizzlies than compete with Mrs. B and her progeny." Buffett regarded it as an ideal business − "one built upon exceptional value to the customer that in turn translates into exceptional economics for its owners." When he bought control, leaving 10 percent with the managing owners and making another 10 percent available as options, Mrs. Blumkin was 90. She continued to work full-time for the business.

Long-term growth

While the Blumkin business was by no means Buffett's first such purchase, it is a model Berkshire acquisition: run by the management that created its success, capable of sustained growth (in the first year sales rose by $14.3 million), low in operating costs, concentrated on an easily understandable business − and cheap. A dollar per dollar of sales is a common rough guide to a buying price: Buffett paid half that much. Growth makes his low prices seem ridiculous: See's Candy Stores, bought in 1972 for $25 million, had operating profits of $62 million in 1998.

The growth in these wholly owned businesses has not been uninterrupted. Every now and

"We have no one – family, recently recruited MBAs etc. – to whom we have promised a chance to run businesses we have bought from owner-managers. And we won't have." *The Essays of Warren Buffett*

again, Buffett has had to tell shareholders of disappointing years. But his long-term view embraces the possibilities of short-term difficulties and set-backs. Only rarely have long-term trends moved against good buys, as with the *Buffalo Evening News*, bought in 1977, which could not escape the adverse change in newspaper economics two decades later. Even the *News*, though, has continued to perform well by most standards, enhancing Buffett's belief in his ability not only to pick but ultimately to manage good acquisitions.

Through his experiences, Buffett developed a strong and simple philosophy for the control and direction of subsidiary companies. The American term for these – "affiliates" – better describes the relationship. As he wrote in 1994, "We achieved our gains through the efforts of a superb corps of operating managers who get extraordinary results from some ordinary-appearing businesses."

3

Avoiding the accounting trap

Using book value and intrinsic business value as accounting tools ● **How both conventional and "creative" accounting can be misleading** ● Using high earnings on equity capital as the main managerial test ● **Calculating "look-through" earnings as the true measure of "economic well-being"** ● Why "economic goodwill" matters more than goodwill in balance sheets ● **The folly of wrapping up silly purchases with accounting niceties** ● "Whatever the merits of options... their accounting treatment is outrageous"

Much of Berkshire Hathaway's remarkable creation of wealth has been built on Buffett's iconoclastic approach to accounting. His unorthodox attitude centers around the use of two concepts: "book value" and "intrinsic business value." As Buffett defines them:

> "Book value is an accounting concept, recording the accumulated financial input from both contributed capital and retained earnings. Intrinsic business value is an economic concept, estimating future cash output discounted to present value. Book value tells you what has been put in; intrinsic business value estimates what can be taken out."

Using book value as a yardstick

Buffett's reports to shareholders always emphasize the annual increase in Berkshire's book value, even though he states that "We never take the one-year figure very seriously." He asks rhetorically, "Why should the time required for a planet to circle the sun synchronize precisely with the time required for business actions to pay off?" He recommends that no less than a five-year view should be taken as "a rough yardstick" of the economic performance of a business.

Buffett calculates this progress in terms of book value "because in our case (although not, by any means, in all cases) it is a conservative but reasonably adequate proxy for growth in intrinsic business value – the measurement that really counts." Although Buffett does not go so far as to claim that his "proxy" gives an accurate figure, book value is very easy to calculate and it also avoids "the subjective (but important) judgments employed in calculation of intrinsic business value."

He explains the difference with a simple analogy. Two students go to college. The book value of their education – the amount spent on fees, and so on – is identical. "But the present value of the future payoff (the intrinsic business value) might vary enormously – from zero to many times the cost of the education." The accountants measure only the first of these figures, although the second is far more important in assessing the worth of the enterprise.

Criticizing the accountants

Unsurprisingly, Buffett is deeply skeptical about conventional accounting – both its use and its misuse. Here he cites a brilliant passage from an unpublished satire by his mentor Benjamin Graham. In 1936, Graham showed how the finances of a real corporation, US Steel, could be utterly transformed by adopting so-called "creative" accounting, operating within the conventions of the profession, but exploiting them to present the company's performance in the most favorable light. Graham wrote:

"Our company has lagged somewhat behind other American business enterprises in utilizing certain advanced bookkeeping methods, by means of which the earning power may be phenomenally enhanced

"Clearly, investors must always keep their guard up and use accounting numbers as a beginning, not an end, in their attempts to calculate true 'economic earnings' accruing to them."
The Essays of Warren Buffett

without requiring any cash outlay or any changes in operating or sales conditions. It has been decided not only to adopt these newer methods but to develop them to a still higher stage of perfection."

Among other devices, plant would be carried on the books at a negative figure, everybody would be paid in stock (thus eliminating the wage bill), and inventory would be valued at virtually nothing. The corporation would thus have "an enormous competitive advantage... We shall be able to sell our products at exceedingly low prices and still show a handsome margin of profit." If competitors sought to imitate its methods, US Steel would devise still more advanced bookkeeping methods and reinforce its "unique prestige... as the originator and pioneer in these new fields of service to the user of steel."

Determining real value

The US Steel satire drives home Buffett's view that accounts and accountants often diverge sharply from the realities of industry and commerce. Even conventional, uncreative accounting can be deeply misleading. It does not provide the two financial yardsticks that Buffett applies when valuing a company:

- Roughly speaking, how much is the business worth? This relates not to its balance sheet but to its intrinsic value.
- How great is its ability to meet future obligations? (For this purpose, it is not enough to calculate cashflow in the orthodox manner. You have to subtract from profits, etc. the amount of the reinvestment in the business that you must make "to fully maintain its long-term competitive position and its unit volume.")

There is a third yardstick, which is non-financial: how effective are the company's managers at operating the business? Buffett argues as follows: "The primary test of managerial economic performance is the achievement of a high earnings rate on equity capital employed (without undue leverage, accounting gimmickry, etc.) and *not the achievement of consistent gains in earnings per share*" [my italics]. The latter criterion has been the prime measure used by stock market analysts and the investors who they serve. As Buffett points out, however, while the "term 'earnings' has a precise ring to it… in reality… earnings can be as pliable as putty when a charlatan heads the company reporting them."

The implication is that there are many charlatans around. "Indeed, some important American fortunes have been created by the monetization of accounting mirages." Excesses similar to those that Graham lampooned in the US Steel satire "have many times since found their way into the financial statements of major American corporations and been duly certified by big-name auditors." Berkshire, naturally, is innocent of these devices. Nevertheless, its own reported earnings are also misleading, although "in a different but important way."

Reporting accurate earnings

What Buffett calls "look-through earnings" give a much more accurate picture of what Berkshire actually earns. The company owns some businesses fully, so all their earnings come into the corporate total. The same is true of Berkshire's share of earnings in all holdings of 50 percent or more and most of those above 20 percent. Below that level, only dividends can be counted. "But while our reported operating earnings reflect only the dividends received, our economic well-being is determined by [the] earnings, not [the] dividends." Conventional accounting allows less than half of Berkshire's earnings "iceberg" to "appear above the surface, in plain view."

"I believe the best way to think about our earnings is in terms of 'look-through' results, calculated as follows: Take $250 million, which is roughly our share of the 1990 operating earnings retained by our investees; subtract $30 million, for the incremental taxes we would have owed had that $250 million been paid to us in dividends; and add the remainder, $220 million, to our reported operating earnings of $371 million. Thus our 1990 'look-through earnings' were about $590 million."

Any practitioner of creative accounting, as deplored by Buffett, would be proud of that piece of multiplication. But he introduces an important qualification. The underlying earnings concerned have been reinvested in the businesses. Their value "is not determined by whether we own 100 percent, 50 percent, 20 percent or 1 percent of the businesses in which they reside". Rather, the value is determined "by the use to which they [the earnings] are put and the subsequent level of earnings produced by that usage." As Buffett admits, this attitude is rather unconventional:

"Many businesses would be better understood by their shareholder owners... if managements and financial analysts modified the primary emphasis they place upon earnings per share, and upon yearly changes in that figure."
The Essays of Warren Buffett

"But we would rather have earnings for which we did not get accounting credit put to good use in a 10 percent-owned company by a management we did not personally hire, than have earnings for which we did get credit put into projects of more dubious potential by another management – even if we are that management."

Creating economic benefit

He is proud of the fact that shareholders in Berkshire have "benefited economically in full measure from your share of our retained earnings, no matter what your accounting system." However, in "a great many capital-intensive businesses," retained earnings that were "credited fully and with painstaking precision... under standard accounting methods have resulted in minor or zero economic value." Buffett stresses that "managers and investors alike must understand that accounting numbers are the beginning, not the end, of business valuation."

Although Buffett comes across as a severe critic of standard accounting procedures, he is at pains to soften this attitude: "We would not like to have the job of designing a better system," and "it's much easier to criticize than to improve... accounting rules. (The inherent problems are monumental.)" His point is rather to stress that investors (and companies) should seek to maximize "economic" earnings, whatever the impact on "accounting" earnings, and to show that focusing on "look-through earnings" is one way to achieve that maximization.

"An approach of this kind will force the investor to think about long-term business prospects rather than short-term stock market prospects, a perspective likely to improve results. It's true, of course, that, in the long run, the scoreboard for investment decisions is market price. But prices will be determined by future earnings. In investing, just as in baseball, to put runs on the scoreboard one must watch the playing field...."

Goodwill accounting

Buffett has occasionally changed his mind about accounting concepts, for example, "goodwill." There are two varieties of goodwill in Berkshire's accounts. One is financial: the difference in value between the market price of shares owned by the company and their value stated under standard accounting principles. The other and more important goodwill is "economic": the difference between the tangible and intrinsic values of a business. When a business is purchased for more than its accounting or book value, the difference appears in the accounts as goodwill. But Berkshire owns "several businesses that possess economic goodwill... far larger than the accounting goodwill that is carried on our balance sheet."

Although Buffett says that "you can live a full and rewarding life without ever thinking about goodwill and its amortization," in his early days he thought about the subject to considerable effect. Graham taught him "to favor tangible businesses whose value depended largely upon economic goodwill," which caused Buffett "to make many important business mistakes of omission, though relatively few of commission." Buffett quotes John Maynard Keynes to explain his error: "The difficulty lies not in the new ideas but in escaping from the old ones."

Loyalty to Graham and his teachings delayed Buffett's escape, which when it came was complete. "Ultimately, business experience, direct and vicarious, produced my

From customer to owner
Buffett was at first a customer for Executive Jet's "fractional aircraft ownership," which is akin to timeshare villas. He thinks it will be the fastest-growing of all the firms in the Berkshire empire.

present strong preference for businesses that possess large amounts of enduring goodwill and that utilize a minimum of tangible assets." Buffett had come to understand that "the traditional wisdom – long on tradition, short on wisdom" made you believe, wrongly, that you were best protected against inflation by investing in businesses "laden with natural resources, plant and machinery, or other tangible assets."

The value of intangible assets

On the contrary, such corporations tend to have low rates of return, which, at times of inflation, can often only just fund the need of the existing business to keep up with rising prices. Consequently, nothing is "left over for real growth, for distribution to owners, or for acquisition of new businesses." In contrast, many owners of intangible assets of lasting value, which needed little in the way of tangible assets, enjoyed earnings that bounded upward during inflation, enabling them to finance acquisitions with ease. Buffett cites communications as an example of enduring business franchises and little tangible investment.

"During inflation," he concludes, "goodwill is the gift that keeps giving." Once again, however, he refers only to true economic goodwill, and not to spurious accounting goodwill, of which there is plenty around and which is another matter entirely:

> "When an overexcited management purchases a business at a silly price, the... accounting niceties... are observed. Because it can't go anywhere else, the silliness ends up in the goodwill account. Considering the lack of managerial discipline that created the account, under such circumstances it might better be labeled 'No-Will'."

"Businesses logically are worth far more than net tangible assets when they can be expected to produce earnings on such assets considerably in excess of market rates of return. The capitalized value of this excess return is economic goodwill." *The Essays of Warren Buffett*

Buffett notes that these businesses still typically observe "the 40-year ritual" of amortizing, or writing off, the goodwill: "the adrenalin so capitalized," he says acidly, "remains on the books as an 'asset' just as if the acquisition had been a sensible one." Berkshire itself follows this 40-year rule, deducting an equal annual amount from its profits to depreciate the accounting goodwill created by takeover. But the consequences depart very significantly from economic reality. For instance, Buffett paid $25 million for See's Candy Stores in 1972. That was $17 million more than the net tangible assets, but very much below the economic value.

Scorning stock options

When attacking conventional accounting, Buffett reserves most scorn for the subject of stock options. You can see why from an unusual item in the Berkshire accounts after the buy in 1997 of General Re, the largest US reinsurer. Compensation (or executive pay) jumped by $68 million after Berkshire bought control. Buffett emphasized that nobody had been paid any more: "the item does not signal that either Charlie [Munger] or I have experienced a personality change. (He [Munger] still travels coach [economy class].)" Rather, that large sum was the cost of replacing General Re's stock option plan with cash incentives linked to managers' operating results.

The crucial point is that there was no actual cost. Under the conventions, however, cash rewards have to be accounted for, while stock options do not figure in the accounts at all. In effect, "accounting principles offer management a choice: pay employees in one form and count the cost, or pay them in another form and ignore the cost." As Buffett comments, their choice of the latter course of action comes as no great surprise. But options do cost real money. When the holder cashes in the option by buying the shares, he pays the old "at-the-market" price, which dates back to the time of issue. He will "exercise" the option (buying the shares at the old price) only if he can now sell them at a significantly higher price.

Counting the true cost of options

The true cost of stock options to the company is, therefore, the difference (often huge) between the price it receives from the option-holders, and the price for which the company could have sold the same shares at-the-market on the day when the option is exercised. Buffett thinks that properly structured options are an "appropriate, and even ideal, way to compensate and motivate top managers." But he has no doubt that "Whatever the merits of options may be, their accounting treatment is outrageous." He justifies his outrage with a clear analogy:

> "Think for a moment of that $190 million we are going to spend for advertising at GEICO [the insurance business] this year. Suppose that, instead of paying cash for our ads, we paid the media in 10-year, at-the-market Berkshire options. Would anyone then care to argue that Berkshire had not borne a cost for advertising, or should not be charged this cost in its books?"

Buffett's question is unlikely to get any more of an answer than the three he asked a few years earlier: "If options aren't a form of compensation, what are they? If compensation isn't an expense, what is it? And if expenses shouldn't go into the calculation of earnings, where in the world should they go?" The reality is that top managements have a vested interest in a system that boosts their profit figures and conceals the fact that their rewards are costing the shareholders great sums of money.

But Buffett finds even more reason for scorn in "restructurings and merger accounting," where "the behavior of managements has been even worse." He finds the "attitude of disrespect that many executives have today for accurate reporting" to be "a business disgrace." His own insistence on getting as near as humanly possible to the financial realities, however, has not held back Berkshire's progress at all. Rather, that insistence has been a cornerstone of its success.

Ideas into action

- Take at least a five-year view of economic performance.

- Work out the present value of the future payoffs of the business.

- Ask whether the business can meet its future obligations.

- Make each dollar of retained earnings create at least a dollar of market value.

- Focus on long-term business prospects, not on short-term share gains.

- Invest in intangible assets that promise to have lasting tangible value.

- Insist on getting as near as you possibly can to financial reality.

Buying companies

Whether or not you will ever purchase a business, or sell one, the principles, as taught by Warren Buffett, are valuable because you can apply them equally to investing in stocks and to valuing a company as a prospective employee.

Helping managers to win

Buffett has developed a highly effective approach to business management through buying companies and helping their managers to win outstanding results. As with his investing in stocks, Buffett rarely diverts from three clearly articulated principles:

Three Key Principles of Business Purchase
1 Buy good businesses at fair prices.
2 Insist on the seller offering a price.
3 Look for evidence of consistent earning power.

Investment in the broadest sense

Even if you do not become a strict follower of Buffett, always have clear, effective criteria for your investment decisions, and always stick to those guidelines. If you are considering buying part of a business – that is, investing in stocks – study this Masterclass in conjunction with that on pages 28–33 to enhance your abilities and success as an investor.

The principles are also a good guide to whether you should join a particular company. You are, in effect, an investor. You are investing part of your life – your most valuable possession – in the employer. Use the Buffett approach to see whether the company is likely to give you full value in return. Unless it can, look for a better "investment" elsewhere.

When looking for a new employer, people are naturally anxious. Be just as cautious when making any decisions about the value of a company. Buffett, a superb acquirer, has written: "we face the inherent problem that the seller of a business practically always knows far more about it than the buyer." Remember that.

Stick to guidelines

Most managers who buy other companies do far worse than Buffett. That is because they depart from his guidelines, despite their crystal-clear logic. Buffett's advice adds up to a series of "don'ts."

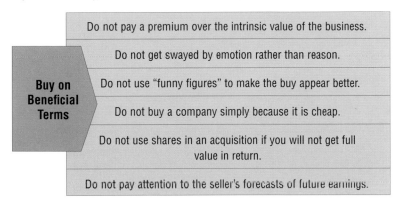

Buy on Beneficial Terms

Do not pay a premium over the intrinsic value of the business.

Do not get swayed by emotion rather than reason.

Do not use "funny figures" to make the buy appear better.

Do not buy a company simply because it is cheap.

Do not use shares in an acquisition if you will not get full value in return.

Do not pay attention to the seller's forecasts of future earnings.

Full obedience to these "don'ts" would prevent most mergers and acquisitions from taking place; Buffett would welcome this. He believes that, however seductive the "strategic" motives, you should buy only on terms that benefit you financially. But truly beneficial deals are hard to find and execute, which is why you should be especially careful.

Measuring motives

There will always be more companies available than you can buy, whatever you can afford. You must also consider management capability; it is all too easy to "bite off more than you can chew." You will rarely find that mergers and acquisitions go as smoothly as you hoped, or yield all the financial benefits that were expected by the time they were expected. So, what are your motives?:

■ Do you find making this deal more fun than running the business, and is that why you are interested?

■ Are you pursuing the deal because you have a strategic purpose in mind?

■ If so, how exactly will achieving that purpose enhance the intrinsic value of the business?

■ If not, why are you considering the deal at all?

1 Assessing management

When considering whether to buy a business, Buffett, not surprisingly, looks for managers who are much like himself. That naturally makes it much easier for him to "like, trust, and admire" them, which he regards as three necessities.

Essential qualities of a manager

To earn Buffett's liking, trust, and respect, managers must show that they possess three essential qualities, all of which are exemplified by Buffett. They must be able to live up to the following statements:

- ■ "I am candid with everybody with whom I have dealings – shareholders, colleagues, employees, customers, and others."
- ■ "I am rational in all my management decisions and actions, analyzing every situation dispassionately before deciding on what is best."
- ■ "I resist the 'institutional imperative' – I do what I think is right, rather than what others are doing."

Can you honestly say the same? If not, why not? Write down the reasons, and consider what changes you can make to pass the triple standard. There is no excuse for falling short.

Producing results

When considering a potential purchase, rule out any company with top managers who do not tell the whole truth, who do not think and act logically, or who follow the herd. Then look at the company's track record. Good management should produce good results.

Characteristics of Good Management
Always puts the owners' interests before management's.
Shows consistent increases in sales and profits from operations.
Achieves above-average returns.
Reinvests profits very effectively.
Acts to ensure that long-term growth prospects are favorable and will be achieved.

The quality issue

The quality of financial results is all-important. How were the high return on equity and superior profit margins achieved? Was it through heavy debt? Buffett prefers companies with minimal borrowings, and so should you. Do high margins result from good management or from a monopoly? Assess where the business fits on the price/quality matrix:

The Price/Quality Matrix		
High price/ high quality	Medium price/ high quality	Low price/ high quality
High price/ medium quality	Medium price/ medium quality	Low price/ medium quality
High price/ low quality	Medium price/ low quality	Low price/ low quality

Only take an interest in companies in which quality is high. High price plus high quality should be profitable, although it is inherently unstable, since it invites competition and narrows the market.

A winning combination

Mrs. Blumkin (see p. 48), with her high quality and low prices, followed a far superior course, widening the market, delighting the customers, and making life very difficult for her competitors. High profits from this valuable combination can flow only from excellent management that follows three golden policies.

The Three Golden Policies		
1 Minimize costs	**2** Maximize sales	**3** Optimize ratio of sales to capital

Following these three golden policies is a sign of well-focused management, guaranteeing a company a high return on equity, high owner-earnings, good margins, and a good return on reinvested capital. Such results all point to a company that will be a good potential investment; it takes good management to mine so much gold, and a good investor to share the mining.

2 Managing managers

How well managers run a business before acquisition must be less important than how they run the company afterward, when it has become your property. To make the most of your purchase, learn the most effective ways of managing the managers.

Establishing trust

When you buy a business, in effect you hire the managers in place. You can take one of three attitudes toward them:

Three Possible Attitudes
1 I do not trust these people to do a proper job, and will replace them with my own nominees.
2 I do not trust these people to do a proper job, but will control them tightly to ensure that they do.
3 I do trust these people to do a proper job, and will let them get on with it in their own way.

For Buffett, the first two attitudes would rule out the acquisition. It rarely makes sense to buy a company whose managers you cannot trust. Ask yourself the following three questions:
- Is this person competent to do the job?
- If "no," why did I keep them?
- If "yes," why am I refusing to let them show their competence?

A policy of non-interference

Buffett does not interfere with a manager's work, *even when he thinks he knows better.* This is crucial. There are two quite separate jobs: running the business, and running the people who do it. Buffett restricts the latter to a very few vital functions, including approval of capital expenditure, approval of top management rewards, and making the top appointments. The key word here is "approval": the managers come up with the plans and you, after due questioning, agree to the idea, revised or not. Ensure your managers tell you bad news as soon as they know it; otherwise they should be free to seek your advice as much or as little as they like.

3 Building the business

Buffett judges a business on its ability to sustain superior organic growth, developing the existing business and markets powerfully, and expanding into new products and geographic areas continuously in ways that enhance the intrinsic value.

Link reward to responsibility

Buffett allows his business managers so much room in which to manage because he wants them to build the business as if it were their own. Top managers often pay lip-service to this idea, but the reality is very different. Rewards, like stock options and bonuses, tend to be linked to the performance of the whole company. Buffett argues that nobody should be rewarded for results that are outside his or her control. If people create greater wealth from their direct responsibilities, share that wealth with them directly, giving both due reward and the incentive to optimize "organic growth."

Organic growth

Your business can grow in several ways. Does it:

■ Sell more year-by-year to existing customers by:
    (a) increasing demand for existing products and/or services?
    (b) improving existing products and/or services?
    (c) introducing new products and/or services?

■ Sell more year-by-year to new customers by:
    (a) widening the demand for existing products and/or services?
    (b) cashing in on the appeal of improved products and/or services?
    (c) introducing new products and/or services?

Supervise growth by insisting on full, regular financial reports that tell you how the company is performing on the same clear criteria that persuaded you to buy. Never be fuzzy. If everyone knows what is expected of them, then you can safely expect that what you want will be achieved.

Analysis

If you have not answered YES to every part of the above questions, something is wrong. Draw up plans for filling the gaps these answers reveal in your organic growth strategy. It is possible to fill gaps by acquisition, but that only makes sense if you follow Buffett's strict rules of purchase.

4

Managing the managers

Why boards of directors should make managers think and act like owners ● **Applying owner-related principles to the management of a business** ● The company as a conduit through which shareholders own the assets ● **Why the word "long-term" gives directors "a lot of wiggle room"** ● The supreme irony of inadequate CEOs who keep their jobs ● **The triple test for CEOs and other corporate seniors** ● Controlling managers by getting people to swim purposefully forward in the same direction

Buffett's approach to management, like his theories on investment, is based on elementary, commonsense principles, such as being rational and candid with shareholders. Berkshire Hathaway's own annual reports have long been prized for their candor, as well as their wisdom and wit. Buffett even seems to find an ironic pleasure in owning up to his failures in these reports, and also at shareholders' meetings. That is explained partly by his belief that confession is good for both the soul and for the company; the public disclosure of error encourages managements to avoid its repetition.

Observation and the laws of probability alike confirm that making mistakes, both large and small, is an inevitable fact of business life. Trying to hide those mistakes, though, can and must be avoided. An error that Buffett especially condemns is the mishandling of the company's funds, which belong not to managers but to shareholders. The prime responsibility of management is looking after the shareholders' capital. That being so, the correct course of action for boards of directors is to make managers think and act like owners themselves.

Buffett believes that such managerial behavior cannot be achieved by regulation. Although he recognizes that on occasions the interests of shareholders and managers will

---

"We won't 'smooth' out quarterly or annual results: If earnings figures are lumpy when they reach headquarters, they will be lumpy when they reach you... I try to give shareholders as much value-defining information as can be conveyed...." *The Essays of Warren Buffett*

clash, he does not agree that legal constraints are effective ways of resolving the conflict. The effective solution is to select the right CEOs in the first place – those who are able, honest, and hard working – and to reward them only for genuine achievement.

Measuring achievement

Buffett measures genuine achievement primarily by return on capital, arguing that managements with higher-than-average ability will prove their ability by earning higher-than-average returns. This justifies the reinvestment of those earnings in ways that give the shareholders more for their money than they could expect to earn by their own efforts. If management cannot pass this acid test, there are only three theoretical options for the management to consider:

- Invest the profits at inferior rates of return.
- Acquire other businesses to enhance performance.
- Give back the money to shareholders and allow them to seek a better, more rewarding home for their funds.

The first option is a nonstarter as it mistreats the shareholders and their money. The second route is, of course, only another way of investing the shareholders' capital; and why should shareholders expect a management that earns lower-than-average returns on its own business to have any success at picking, buying, or running higher-than-average companies? That leaves only the third option. Buffett totally agrees with the management guru Peter Drucker that companies have no right to retain funds that they cannot put to excellent use.

The "Owner's Manual"

Managements will more effectively focus on giving shareholders better returns on their investment if they master what Buffett calls "owner-related business principles." These appear in what he terms the "Owner's Manual," which, while clearly relating specifically to Berkshire, also establishes a dozen general principles:

- Think of shareholders as owner-partners, and of yourselves as managing partners.
- Have a major portion of your net worth invested in the company ("We eat our own cooking").
- Aim to maximize the average annual rate of gain in intrinsic business value on a [growth in value] per-share basis.
- For preference, reach your goal by directly owning a diversified group of businesses that generate cash and consistently earn above-average returns on capital.
- Ignore conventional accounting, with its insistence on consolidating the earnings of individual companies, and concentrate on their individual earnings.
- Do not let accounting consequences influence your decisions on operations or allocating capital.
- Use debt sparingly and, when you do have to borrow, try to structure your loans over a long term at a fixed rate of interest.
- Never ignore long-term economic consequences for the shareholders when buying businesses. (Buffett refers to the sinful opposite as "filling a managerial wish list at shareholder expense.")
- Check noble intentions periodically against results – does every dollar of retained earnings over time deliver at least a dollar of market value?

- Only issue shares when you receive as much in business value as you give.
- Regardless of the price you may be offered, never sell any good businesses.
- Be candid in reporting to shareholders, emphasizing the plusses and minuses that are important in appraising business value.

Learning from the great
Buffett is a follower of the great Cambridge economist and investor John Maynard Keynes, who seldom invested at any one time in more than two or three companies in which he had full confidence.

There is a 13th principle established in the "Owner's Manual": "We would rather see Berkshire Hathaway's stock at a fair level than a high level."

Like the others, this principle is full of common sense and the lessons of experience. There is a weakness to the 13 principles, however, which is that few managers are in the same fortunate position as Buffett and Munger (Buffett's long-time friend), who were not only managing partners but also controlling partners thanks to the size of their shareholdings. Massive stock options and other means of making managers into multimillionaire shareholders still leave these hired hands with minute fractions of the total equity. They have a tendency to think of these holdings as stakes in the company itself, and fail to grasp a central point stressed by Buffett: "We do not view the company itself as the ultimate owner of our business assets but instead view the company as a conduit through which our shareholders own the assets."

Providing information

Buffett and Munger, after all, could have owned these assets directly, instead of placing them in Berkshire. Hired-hand executives, however large their fortunes may be, clearly never have this option. But the mind-set recommended by Buffett has an important consequence and benefit. The owner of a private company managed by other people expects regular and full information about what is going on and how the management evaluates the business, currently and prospectively: "you should expect no less in a public company." The shareholders are entitled to the same sort of reporting that "we feel is owed to us by managers of our business units."

This full provision of full information is not the norm for the majority of publicly owned companies. Buffett points out, however, that such companies differ from each other in fundamental ways that are not acknowledged by most commentators. According to Buffett, there are three categories: first, and by far the most common, is where the corporation has no controlling shareholder; second, as in Berkshire's case, where the controlling owner is also the manager; and, in the third case, where the controlling owner is not involved in the management.

The last two cases are so rare that little can be said of great general value. As Buffett says, where somebody has both ownership and management control, even if he is "mediocre or worse — or is overreaching — there is little a director can do about it except object." The third case, however, should logically be the most effective in ensuring first-class management:

> "... the owner is neither judging himself nor burdened with the problem of garnering a majority. He can also ensure that outside directors are selected who will bring useful qualities to the board. These directors, in turn, will know that the good advice they give will reach the right ears, rather than being stifled by a recalcitrant management. If the controlling

"The management failings that Charlie and I have seen make us thankful that we are linked with the managers of our three permanent holdings. They love their business, they think like owners, and they exude integrity and ability."
The Essays of Warren Buffett

owner is intelligent and self-confident, he will make decisions in respect to management that are meritocratic and pro-shareholder. Moreover — and this is critically important — he can readily correct any mistake he makes."

As the passage above suggests, Buffett is by no means optimistic about getting similar responses in a company that does not have a controlling shareholder. He believes that "directors should behave as if there is a single absentee owner, whose long-term interest they should try to further in all proper ways." But what if they behave otherwise? As Buffett points out, the word "long-term" gives directors "a lot of wiggle room":

"If they lack either integrity or the ability to think independently, directors can do great violence to shareholders while still claiming to be acting in their long-term interest. But assume the board is functioning well and must deal with a management that is mediocre or worse. Directors then have the responsibility for changing that management, just as an intelligent owner would do if he were present. And if able but greedy managers overreach and try to dip too deeply into the shareholders' pockets, directors must slap their hands."

Criticizing the CEO

Buffett remarks that there are companies where "CEOs clearly do not belong in the jobs" although "their positions, nevertheless, are usually secure." But security should depend on performance. Buffett places very highly the attraction and retention of outstanding executives; and at Berkshire, he observes, this task "hasn't been all that difficult." Buffett compares the performance of CEOs in his own businesses with that of "many CEOs" elsewhere, and finds that it "contrasts vividly."

The "supreme irony of business management," he writes, is that "it is far easier for an inadequate CEO to keep his job" than for an inadequate subordinate to do so. Buffett cites in proof the fate of secretaries whose typing is too slow or salesmen who fail to sell. The CEO benefits from having a job that, unlike typing or selling, usually has no performance standards. Where they do exist, the standards for the CEO are "often fuzzy or they may be waived or explained away, even when the performance shortfalls are major and repeated. At too many companies, the boss shoots the arrow of managerial performance and then hastily paints the bullseye around the spot where it lands."

Buffett pinpoints another "important, but seldom recognized, distinction between the boss and the foot soldier." The CEO "has no immediate superior whose performance is itself getting measured." The board of directors ostensibly fulfills that role of superior, but "seldom measures itself and is infrequently held to account for substandard corporate performance. If the Board makes a mistake in hiring, and perpetuates that mistake, so what?"

"As a company with a major communications business, it would be inexcusable for us to apply lesser standards of accuracy... when reporting on ourselves than we would expect our news people to apply when reporting on others." *The Essays of Warren Buffett*

The excellent CEO

No doubt drawing on his own considerable boardroom experience, Buffett notes that "relations between the Board and the CEO are expected to be congenial. At board meetings, criticism of the CEO's performance is often viewed as the social equivalent of belching." He softens his

The supreme CEO
Buying seven percent of Coca-Cola gave Buffett an insider's view of the brilliant performance of its late CEO, Roberto Goizueta (left). His successor, Doug Ivester, found the going much harder.

criticism by observing that most CEOs and directors are "able and hard-working and a number are truly outstanding." But, in fact, rather few can pass his triple test: that they should "love their businesses... think like owners and... exude integrity and ability."

Why has it been not "all that difficult" for Buffett to find such people? The great majority of his managers came in with businesses that Buffett bought because of their outstanding record. On the face of it, if the record is outstanding, so is the manager. These people, moreover, think like owners because they have been owners. Buffett's management theory is akin to John Huston's approach to directing films: if you cast the right actors, the film will almost certainly look after itself.

As Buffett puts it, "They were managerial stars long before they knew us, and our main contribution has been to not get in their way." Because these are able managers of high character running businesses about which they are passionate, there is no need for demanding, intensive supervision: "You can have a dozen or more reporting to you and still have time for an afternoon nap."

Criticizing stock options

Buffett is just as frank (and heretical) about giving managers stock options. He says flatly that:

"When the result is equitable, it is accidental. Once granted, the option is blind to individual performance, and because it is irrevocable and unconditional (so long as a manager stays in the company), the sluggard receives rewards from his options precisely as does the star. A managerial Rip Van Winkle, ready to doze for 10 years, could not wish for a better 'incentive' system."

His criticism of stock options is based on the following:

- Stock options are inevitably tied to the overall performance of a corporation. Logically, therefore, they should be awarded only to those managers with overall responsibility. Managers with limited areas of responsibility should have incentives that pay off in relation to results under their control.
- Options should be priced at "true business value" and should not reward managers for plowing back the shareholders' own money.
- Incentive-compensation systems should reward key managers only "for meeting targets in their own bailiwicks." At Berkshire, this can mean incentive bonuses of five times base salary, if not more.

Despite this generous attitude toward his own executives, Buffett displays a puritanical strain in his attitude to managers and their remuneration, although he would prefer the description "rational" to puritanical. A remarkable passage in one of his annual reports sums up his views:

"At Berkshire, only Charlie and I have the managerial responsibility for the entire business. Therefore, we are the only parties who should logically be

"Except in highly unusual cases, owners are not well served by the sale of part of their business at a bargain price – whether the sale is to outsiders or insiders. The obvious conclusion: options should be priced at true business value."
The Essays of Warren Buffett

compensated on the basis of what the enterprise does as a whole. Even so, that is not a compensation arrangement we desire. We have carefully designed both the company and our jobs so that we do things we enjoy with people we like."

Work as pleasure

Buffett and Munger enjoy their work to the full. They cite Ronald Reagan's dictum: hard work never killed anybody, but why risk it? The pair, said Buffett, were "delighted" with their "cushy" jobs.

It is just as important to Buffett that "we are forced to do very few boring or unpleasant tasks." The pair also benefit from "the abundant array of material and psychic perks that flow to the heads of corporations." They do not "under such idyllic conditions... expect shareholders to ante up loads of compensation for which we have no possible need." That leads to an honest conclusion to which few other top managers would subscribe (not out loud, that is): "Indeed, if we were not paid at all, Charlie and I would be delighted with the cushy jobs we hold. At bottom, we subscribe to Ronald Reagan's creed: 'It's probably true that hard work never killed anyone, but I figure why take the chance.'"

Determined delegation

The "cushiness" results from Buffett's determined pursuit of delegation. In any case, the head office is too small to interfere across so large an empire. He once commented that he had expanded the office to 12.8 people: a new employee only worked a four-day week. He is by no means uncritical, however, saying that, "With almost every one of the companies Berkshire owns, I think I would do something different if I were running them – in some cases substantially different."

Yet he resists the temptation to interfere. Although he watches the figures for Berkshire's companies like the proverbial hawk, he usually waits for managers to contact him, rather than the other way around, telling his people:

"All of you do a first-class job in running your own operations with your own individual styles. We are going to keep it that way. You can talk to me about what is going on as little or as much as you wish with only one caveat. If there is significant bad news, let me know early."

The best measure of the strength of Buffett's ideas on managerial control, and of their application in practice, is that really bad news has been rare, and certainly much less common than in the majority of companies which are controlled in a far more bureaucratic and hierarchical manner. Buffett has a laconic way of describing his very different attitude: "I sort of accept things as they come." That is because his philosophies ensure that things come the right way and come out right.

Ideas into action

■ Demonstrate higher-than-average ability by earning higher-than-average returns.

■ Think of shareholders as owner-partners and yourself as a managing partner.

■ Do not view the company as the owner of its assets.

■ Try to further the long-term interest of shareholders at all times.

■ Set clear performance standards for everybody, including the boss.

■ Tie rewards only to results under a manager's own control.

■ Let managers run their own operations in their own styles.

Transforming Berkshire Hathaway

Buffett began his move from obscurity in Omaha to world fame by abandoning success and inviting failure. After running the Buffett partnership with phenomenal success for some 13 years, he closed it down in 1969.

A few years earlier he had bought into a cheap textile company named Berkshire Hathaway. It was one of his biggest mistakes. "We went into a terrible business because it was cheap." The problems were plainly visible. Over nine years Berkshire had lost $10 million on sales of $530 million. Despite good management and a cooperative workforce, Buffett could not achieve success even after years of effort. After 1979 Berkshire "consumed major amounts of cash. By mid-1985, it became clear, even to me, that this condition was almost sure to continue."

The textile operation was at long last closed down. But success came out of failure. Very early on, in 1967, "cash generated by the textile operation was used to fund our entry into insurance." That proved to be the catalyst for Buffett's breakthrough. Insurance has been a powerful engine behind Berkshire's expansion – a prime explanation for a growth in book value per Berkshire share from $19.46 in 1964 to nearly $20,000 in 1997 – when the market valuation of the entire company passed $50 billion.

Insurance goldmines

Buffett's discovery of the joys of insurance long pre-dated his Berkshire purchase. As a student of Benjamin Graham, Buffett found that his hero was chairman of GEICO (Government Employees Insurance Company), "to me an unknown company in an unfamiliar industry." Buffett took a train to Washington, DC, to visit the company and got a four-hour lecture in insurance from a man who later became CEO, and who made Buffett "more excited about GEICO than I have ever been about a stock." He both bought and sold the shares – and much later, in 1976, started building a large position in the company. Berkshire's first third of GEICO cost $45.7 million; its final purchase of half cost the firm $2.3 billion. That is a measure of how richly the original investment had paid off.

With their funds invested in stocks chosen on the same principles as those for the old Buffett partnership, the insurance companies have been Buffett's goldmines. By 1999, the original buys had become the nucleus for an insurance group with revenues of $13.6 billion, and an operating profit of $1.24 billion.

If Berkshire had invested only in insurance, it would have been among America's most rewarding stocks. But Buffett learned to combine two apparently contradictory policies: vulnerability and spread of risk. Because he took huge positions (for example, in catastrophe insurance), Berkshire was vulnerable to bad performance in any of them. But he

"Should you find yourself in a chronically leaking boat, energy devoted to changing vessels is likely to be more productive than energy devoted to patching leaks." *The Essays of Warren Buffett*

spread his risks by building the group on three separate foundations: insurance, publicly held stocks, and widely diversified, privately owned businesses. Berkshire was neither strictly a conglomerate (a holding company for various active interests), nor an investment trust, nor an insurance group. It was all three of those things at once.

Using reason

*T*he person who always acts impetuously, illogically, unfairly, and obstinately is most unlikely to succeed in any activity. Assess how rational you are and take action to let your head rule your decisions and their implementation.

How rational are you?

The most important word in Buffett's vocabulary is "why." He always strives to discover the reason "why" things happen, "why" he should do some things, and not others, "why" one approach is better than another. Can you live up to his standards of rationality? Look at the following seven statements. Give yourself a score on a scale of zero to 10. You score zero for "I never think before acting," 5 for "I sometimes think," and 10 for "I always do."

- ■ I think before acting.
- ■ I have a logical justification for my actions and beliefs.
- ■ I do not stop my inquiries until I am as certain as possible that I know the truth.
- ■ I understand my emotions, but never allow them to determine my behavior.
- ■ I strive to be fair in my dealings with others.
- ■ I change my mind if other people, or new facts, show that I am wrong.
- ■ I set out my arguments clearly and logically, so that others can follow them.

Using a checklist

Write down these seven statements on a card, and refer to them when working on anything to see if you are leaving the road of reason. Ask yourself every evening what you have done to harness the power of reason, and (using Buffett's metaphor) to get maximum output from your motor.

Analysis

- ■ A score between 25 and 45 shows that you are a reasonable person but that some of the time you act unreasonably.
- ■ Follow a rational course of action and improve on that unsatisfactory performance.
- ■ Concentrate on the points of major weakness and find one simple way of correcting each fault.

1 Breaking the habit

Buffett believes that bad habits, such as irrational behavior, are not inborn but are developed at a young age, and become harder to dislodge with advancing years. Use the checklist on page 88 as a way of breaking poor intellectual habits that prevent rational behavior.

Stuck in their ways

Middle-aged managers are frequently guilty of stubbornly refusing to make changes that would provide great benefits, and even avert disaster. They become stuck in a mental habit or "mind-set." These fixed attitudes are often revealed in ritual phrases, such as:

- "That's not the way we do things around here."
- "If that is such a good idea, why isn't anybody else doing it?"
- "That's been tried before, and it didn't work."

Reject such statements as denials of rationality. They prevent serious, rational investigation that might lead to change for people who irrationally prefer an unsatisfactory status quo.

Develop your strengths

Whatever your age, welcome positive change and use Buffett's "role model" plan to align your performance to that of your hero. There is no reason why even old dogs cannot learn new tricks.

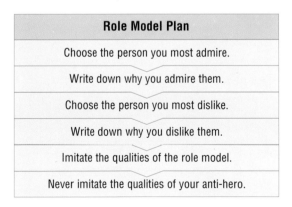

Role Model Plan
Choose the person you most admire.
Write down why you admire them.
Choose the person you most dislike.
Write down why you dislike them.
Imitate the qualities of the role model.
Never imitate the qualities of your anti-hero.

Role models are useful for everybody, but always remember that you have innate and unique strengths and weaknesses; only an identical twin has the same genes. Your genetic inheritance determines your personality as well as your physique. You can improve both with practice and techniques as long as you are honest with yourself about your qualities. Try to be objective and seek to build on your strengths and minimize your weaknesses.

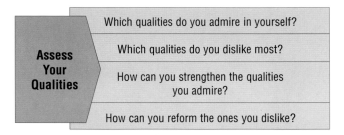

Assess Your Qualities	Which qualities do you admire in yourself?
	Which qualities do you dislike most?
	How can you strengthen the qualities you admire?
	How can you reform the ones you dislike?

Be positive

Being completely honest about yourself is not always easy, especially when it comes to acknowledging your weaknesses. But do not turn inherited difficulties into impossibilities. It is all too tempting to allow what you consider a flaw in your personality or a weakness in your intellect to prevent you from achieving a desired goal. Remember that:

- The fact that you find learning foreign languages difficult does not mean that you cannot learn one.
- The fact that financial figuring comes hard does not mean that you cannot master accounts, budgets, and balance sheets.
- The fact that you often act impulsively and emotionally does not mean that you cannot learn to act rationally at all, or at least most, times.

Overcoming Your Weaknesses

Slow learners need more time, but, if allowed, they can learn well enough to excel. Taking your weak areas as opportunities can turn them into strengths.

The owner-manager of a company wanted to hand over management to his top-performing sales director who was "figure-blind." So, the boss made the director draw up budgets and management accounts, even though this resulted in lost sales revenue while the man wrestled with the figures. But he learned, and made a fortune for his old boss as a manager whose grasp of accounts became one of his key strengths.

2 Mastering emotions

You may feel that rationality cannot extend to the emotions. You cannot control your feelings: for example, you either like somebody or you do not; something either makes you angry or it does not. But you can learn to control the expression of that feeling.

Placing emotion under control
Buffett will work only with people he likes, but he makes sure that his liking does not prevent objective judgment of those people, or objective action if they let him down. No doubt, Buffett is sometimes angry. But does he allow anger to influence his decisions or his behavior? People often place their anger under control. For example, if another driver cuts you up in traffic, you will react angrily to a stranger, but very differently if the driver is your boss.

Dealing with anger
If you are angry, ask: "What purpose will my anger serve?" Usually, anger arises because somebody else is not behaving in the way that you want. Will your anger help to change their behavior? Probably not. You may think that "letting off steam" is good for you; but, in reality, it is an unpleasant condition that any rational person would try to avoid. Far better not to get angry in the first place, but if you do, subdue it swiftly by applying the four-point anger analysis plan:

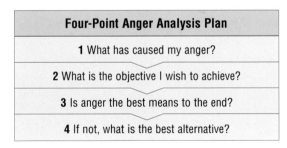

Four-Point Anger Analysis Plan
1 What has caused my anger?
2 What is the objective I wish to achieve?
3 Is anger the best means to the end?
4 If not, what is the best alternative?

The cause of anger is often a *fait accompli*: a mistake has been made, say, and cannot be unmade. The uncontrolled emotion therefore serves no useful purpose. Equally, if you made the mistake yourself, the emotion of guilt is also useless, as it will neither correct the error nor help you to avoid making the same mistake in future.

3 Learning from mistakes

Buffett's attitude to error is among the most important aspects of his teaching. Expect to make mistakes sometimes and, if they occur, analyze the reason for them. Use the analysis to avoid the worse mistake: doing it again.

Accepting error

True rationality accepts that mistakes will happen, and it is deeply irrational to suppose that you have been, ever will be, or ever can be without fault. Every time you buy a stock, for example, you make a mistake; there is always another investment that will perform better than your choice. Buffett's avoidance of high-technology stocks, for instance, sounds reasonable because it is rational to invest only in businesses that you understand. But, ironically, Berkshire Hathaway's amazing record would actually have been better if Buffett had invested in Microsoft, and nothing else.

Analyzing your mistakes

The irrational response to error is to try to rewrite history; "if only I had..." is a familiar cry. Instead of being defeatist, analyze your mistakes. Once you have established the reasons why something has gone wrong, it is relatively easy to make sure you do not repeat the mistakes. Ask yourself the following seven questions:

■ Did I lack adequate information about the present?
■ Did I make an inaccurate prediction?
■ Is this a mistake I have made before?
■ Did I ignore logical lessons that I already knew?
■ Does what happened teach me a new lesson?
■ Did I do the wrong thing?
■ Did I do the right thing in the wrong way?

Buffett's mistaken sale of shares in McDonald's in 1998, for example, was based on an inaccurate reading of the company's poor US sales figures, from which he predicted, possibly incorrectly, that its growth prospects had fallen below his requirements. Such mistakes have been rare in Berkshire's history because of Buffett's logical insistence on keeping stock indefinitely, knowing that bad short-term patches do not invalidate good long-term analysis.

WARREN BUFFETT

Stick to your principles

In other words, Buffett ignored his own teaching. The advice given by Polonius to Laertes in *Hamlet* is particularly sound: "To thine own self be true." Many mistakes flow from aberrations that override this principle. The aberrations often stem from following conventional wisdom rather than your own (or, indeed, Buffett's). As an investor, have the courage to obey at all times the five rational principles expounded by Buffett:

Five Rational Principles
1 Focus on a few things, not many things.
2 Ignore short-term fluctuations, unless they invalidate your long-term expectations.
3 Do not believe that booms will continue forever, or that slumps will never end.
4 If you have done your homework thoroughly, have the courage of your convictions.
5 Be as ruthless when analyzing your success as you are when analyzing failure.

Analyzing your successes

You can learn from your successes as well as your failures. Subject them to the same scrutiny as your mistakes, and learn from them. People tend to pride themselves on their success and take it as proof of their brilliance. But success is often accompanied by serious mistakes that might have proved fatal. Ask yourself:

- Did you succeed in spite of your ignorance about the present and the future?
- Did success flow from repeating previous experience, or breaking into new ground?
- Did you do the right thing in the wrong way, but succeed because the thing was so right that your mistakes did not affect the outcome?

Reason is a hard master, but one whose lessons, like Buffett's, always repay intelligent obedience.

5

Applying the power of reason

How rationality determines the effectiveness of intelligence and talent ● **Counting the cost of bad decisions, including errors of omission** ● Using reason, not to predict, but to measure predictability ● **"Margin of safety": the difference between price and value** ● Ensuring that increases in earnings outstrip increases in capital employed ● **Three rational ways to learn from failure and create success** ● Limiting yourself to what you – and you alone – can do

Buffett believes that the secret of his business success lies not with higher intelligence but with the effective use of that intelligence, that is, the application of reason. To him, "the big thing" is always rationality, and the greater the rationality, the greater the effectiveness. As long as they follow the rational course, everybody "has the ability absolutely to do anything I do and much beyond." He looks at IQ and talent as representing the horsepower of the motor. The output, however, is "the efficiency with which that motor works" and that depends on rationality: "A lot of people start out with 400-horsepower motors but only get a hundred horsepower of output. It's way better to have a 200-horsepower motor and get it all into output."

Developing good habits

But this raises an important question: "Why do smart people do things that interfere with getting the output they're entitled to?" Buffett's explanation is that behaving irrationally gets embedded into the habits and character and temperament. So failure to achieve will arise "because you get in your own way, not because the world doesn't allow you." The bad habits are not inborn, in Buffett's view. Rather, they develop over time. This is an insidious process: the "chains of habit are too light to be felt until they are too heavy to be broken." So, he advises young people to work on their habits from the start:

> "Pick out the person you admire the most, and then write down why you admire them. Then put down the person that, frankly, you can stand the least, and write down the qualities that turn you off in that person. The qualities of the one you admire are traits that

you, with a little practice, can make your own, and that, if practiced, will become habit-forming. Look at... what you find really reprehensible in others and decide that those are things you are not going to do. If you do that, you'll find you convert all of your own horsepower into output."

The personalization of issues is a constant theme in Buffett's thinking and practice. In his mind, figures are much less important than people. As he points out: "I have turned down business deals that were otherwise decent because I didn't like the people I would have to work with." Such an attitude may appear overemotional, but Buffett regards his approach as highly rational. After all, he reasons, what is the point of working at things you dislike with people you dislike? Not only does he "get to do what I like to do every single day of the year" but he gets "to do it with people I like," in particular, his partner Charlie Munger. During his active years with Berkshire Hathaway, Munger seems to have have acted as Buffett's conscience, and a reminder that he is mortal and fallible: "You have to calibrate with Charlie, though, because Charlie says everything I do is dumb. If he says it's really dumb, I know it is, but if he just says it's dumb, I take that as an affirmative vote."

"We intend... working only with people we like and admire... working with people who cause your stomach to churn seems much like marrying for money – probably a bad idea under any circumstances, but absolute madness if you are already rich."
The Essays of Warren Buffett

Making the wrong decisions

Sometimes Buffett's decisions have indeed been dumb, including the very decision, the purchase of Berkshire Hathaway, that resulted in the most successful investment achievement in business history. "We went into a terrible business because it was cheap." Buffett refers to this as the "used cigar butt" approach to investing. "You see this cigar butt down there, it's soggy and terrible, but there's one puff left, and it's free." Buffett took the decision on rational grounds: Berkshire was selling below the value of its working capital, which was then Buffett's prime criterion, but buying it was still "a terrible, terrible mistake."

It was a mistake of commission. But Buffett's errors ("all kinds of bad decisions that have cost us billions of dollars") have mostly been mistakes of omission. In one case, he actually made a decision to buy, "and I just didn't execute. We would've made many billions of dollars. But we didn't do it." In other cases, he has failed to optimize his profit. As he says, conventional accounting does not record failures of this nature, but reason argues that the cost of lost opportunities, all the same, is no less real.

Following the rational course

Seizing opportunities must be more important than spotting the opening, whether it is specific (the availability of an excellent business at a fair price) or general (a trend, like the long postwar bull market). The best business decision Buffett ever made was to exploit that postwar trend, a general opportunity that was available to anybody, by becoming a professional investor. "It was just jumping in the pool, basically." But his jump was governed from the start by rationality. He worked out, for instance,

One-way street
The background to Buffett's success was the long, fabulous bull market in American stocks from 1965 to the present day. His own key decision, against that backdrop, was "just jumping in the pool."

that "you do not need a great many deals to succeed in the investment business." The rational course is to focus on a few things, not many things.

"In fact, if... you got a punch card with 20 punches on it, and every time you made an investment decision you used up one punch, and that's all you were going to get, you would make 20 very good investment decisions. And you could get very rich, incidentally. You don't need 50 good ideas at all."

The vein of applied rationality runs through all Buffett's actions. For example, he has often been pressed to divide (or split) Berkshire's stock, so that it sells for a less intimidating price than $70,000 (or more) per share. But keeping the price high means that Berkshire attracts "a slightly more long-term oriented group of investors." Buffett thinks that entrepreneurs should prefer shareholders "very much like themselves, with the same time horizons and expectations."

This rational preference, in Berkshire's case, has the very sensible by-product, which is very important to Buffett, of saving time and trouble: "We don't talk about quarterly earnings, we don't have an investor relations department, and we don't have conference calls with Wall Street analysts, because we don't want people who are focusing on what's going to happen next quarter or even next year."

Measuring predictability

Buffett's own focus is famously long-term. Rationality says that you cannot predict the future, and the further out your forecasts stretch, the less accurate they are. But reason also says that you can measure predictability. For instance, Buffett is fully aware today that, "The technological revolution will change the world in dramatic ways, and quickly." Exactly how and when that change will come, though, is beyond Buffett and probably everybody else. That is why he avoids high technology stocks and heads for more "ordinary" businesses.

A reliable shave
Buffett gives Gillette as an example of a predictable company. Because men will still shave, the company is likely to look more or less the same two decades on. Buffett likes an "absence of change."

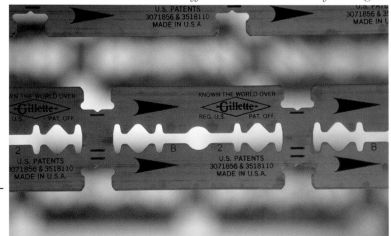

"I look for businesses in which I think I can predict what they're going to look like in 10 or 15 or 20 years. That means businesses that will look more or less as they do today, except that they'll be larger and doing more business internationally... So I focus on an absence of change."

He gives the example of Wrigley's chewing gum: "I don't think the Internet is going to change how people are going to chew gum." Nor does he believe that cyberspace will change the fact that Coke will be "the drink of preference" or affect its gains in global consumption per capita. Gillette is another example. Will the Internet change whether people shave or how they shave? Reason says "No." The event has very low probability and thus very high predictability, and "we are looking for the very predictable."

Reason is the only way to evaluate any financial market place or asset. For example, in 1998, Buffett noted that returns on equity in American business at large were much higher than they were in 1969 or 1974 (two previous highs), or at any other time in history. In valuing the overall market, therefore, the rational question is: "Do you crank in the present 20 percent returns on equity for American business in aggregate and say that's a realistic figure to stick on for this future that runs out until eternity?" Rationally, Buffett called this "a fairly reckless assumption" which does not leave much "margin of safety" and which therefore signals caution.

Searching for value

As noted earlier (see p. 26), Buffett learned about the "margin of safety" from Benjamin Graham at the Columbia Graduate Business School. Graham, another supreme rationalist, taught that price does not equate with value: price is what you pay, and value is what you get. Buffett found that picking stocks with value sounds trickier than it is. For instance, during his early days, leafing through a stock market manual page by page, Buffett found there were several stocks priced at one times earnings, that is, if $10, say, normally purchased $1 of earnings, these shares paid the same for only $1.

Reason told Buffett that this collection of stocks had to include tremendous bargains. "The truth is, you know them when you see them. They're so cheap." You do, however, require clear-sighted rational analysis to confirm your intuition and to establish the vital realities. For example, in 1985, Buffett was mulling over the lessons of three wholly owned businesses: Nebraska Furniture Mart, See's Candy Stores, and the *Buffalo Evening News*. The trio, he reported, had earned $72 million before tax in the previous year, compared to some $8 million 15 years earlier before Berkshire had purchased them. But Buffett still refused to rejoice unreservedly:

> "While an increase in earnings from $8 million to $72 million sounds terrific – and usually is – you should not automatically assume that to be the case. You must first make sure that earnings were not depressed in the base year. If they were instead substantial in relation to capital employed, an even more important point must be examined: how much additional capital was required to produce the additional earnings?"

"We simply attempt to be fearful when others are greedy, and greedy only when others are fearful." Berkshire Hathaway Annual Report, 1986

Testing performance

Berkshire's trio of businesses passed both rational tests with ease. Fifteen years before, all three had earned large amounts on capital. That capital had risen by some $40 million since then, well below the $64 million increase in profit. As Buffett pointed out, the average American business fell markedly short of this performance, requiring about $5 of extra capital to add $1 to its pre-tax earnings. This inspired the rationalist to acerbic comment: "When returns on capital are ordinary, an earn-more-by-putting-up-more record is no great managerial achievement. You can get the same result personally while operating from your rocking chair. Just quadruple the capital you commit to a savings bank and you will quadruple your earnings."

The rationalist seeks to apply meaningful tests to all issues and all achievements to ensure that success is real and reported as accurately as possible. The same is true of failure. Nothing marks out Buffett more distinctively than his honesty about his present and past follies. His letters to shareholders, his interviews, and the like, are peppered with admissions like, "Here I need to make a confession (ugh)... my decision to sell McDonald's was a very big mistake": or, more mildly, "Remember Wagner, whose music has been described as better than it sounds? Well, Berkshire's progress was not as good as it looks."

Buffett almost seems to revel in exposing his follies, not just when they first appear, but again and again. In 1983, for instance, he went right back to the start of his saga: "Charlie and I... controlled three companies, Berkshire Hathaway, Inc., Diversified Retailing Company, Inc., and Blue Chip Stamps, each a single business company, respectively in textiles, department stores, and trading stamps." They were not successful: "These cornerstone businesses (carefully chosen, it should be noted, by your Chairman and Vice Chairman) have, respectively, (1) survived but earned almost nothing, (2) shriveled in size while incurring large losses, and (3) shrunk in sales volume to about 5 percent its size at the time of entry. (Who says 'you can't lose 'em all'?)."

No dividends policy

There is always a rational point to these confessions, however. The passage above occurs in a discussion of dividends, which Buffett does not distribute. His reasoning is that historically Berkshire has obeyed his golden rule: more than $1 of market value has been created for every dollar of earnings reinvested in the business. Therefore, "any distribution would have been contrary to the financial interest of shareholders, large or small." Moreover, because of the poor performance listed above, "significant distributions in the early years might have been disastrous."

If the three companies had paid out in dividends all they earned, "we would almost certainly have no earnings at all now – and perhaps no capital either." Instead, the money was committed to "much better businesses," which was the "only way we were able to overcome those origins." Buffett goes on to comment that, "It's been like overcoming a misspent youth." In other words, Buffett drew three powerful rational conclusions from his triple failure:

- Invest money to earn more for shareholders than they can earn themselves.
- Diversify to spread risks by more than balancing failures with success elsewhere.
- Do not repeat mistakes, but use them as stepping stones to success.

Looking to the future
On Buffett's death, all his Berkshire Hathaway shares will go to his wife, Susan, who sits on the board of directors. If she does not outlive him, the shares will be given to a family foundation.

Berkshire after Buffett

Rational analysis and observation clearly show Buffett that his creation, for all the contribution made by Charlie Munger and others, including the managers of his operating companies, essentially hinges on one man (himself) who is mortal. He makes a point of telling people that he has faced this issue, as rationally, as ever: "I've already sent out a letter that tells what should be done, and I've got another letter that's addressed that will go out at the time, and it starts out 'Yesterday I died,' and then tells what the plans of the company are."

All his shares go to his wife, Susan, if she survives him, or to a foundation if she does not. Berkshire will then be "going forward with a vitally interested, but non-management owner and with a management that must perform for that owner." In theory, that should work well, provided that the "owner" takes the same eminently rational view as Buffett: that you succeed by limiting yourself to what you and you alone can do, and delegate everything else. His own retirement will consequently leave only two functions to be filled, one of which is to allocate capital, which is a straightforward intellectual exercise.

The overwhelmingly obvious fact, however, is that Buffett has allocated capital more successfully by far than any man in history. It is therefore unreasonable, and by no means rational, to suppose that somebody else will do as well. His second role is even more problematical: "to help 15 or 20 senior managers keep a group of people enthused about what they do when they have no financial need whatsoever to do it." He estimates that, "at least three-quarters of the managers that we have are rich beyond any possible financial need."

Fulfilling that second role depends not on the powers of reason alone but on those of empathy and personality. Buffett's unique character, with its combination of humanity and toughness, cold reason and personal warmth,

---

"Lest we end on a morbid note, I also want to assure you that I have never felt better. I love running Berkshire, and if enjoying life promotes longevity, Methuselah's record is in jeopardy."
The Essays of Warren Buffett

is what one business school professor has called "a five-sigma event," meaning a statistical aberration so rare it practically never happens. *Business Week* has commented that "just as no one other than Buffett could have created Berkshire Hathaway, it may well come to pass that no one other than Buffett can make it work."

Ideas into action

- Start as early as possible in your career to develop only good habits.

- Look at what you find really reprehensible, and avoid it.

- Try to do work that you like and only with people you like.

- Focus on a few good things, rather than making many investments.

- Look for businesses whose long-term futures are predictable.

- Confess your serious errors fully to yourself as well as to others.

- Invest money to earn more for shareholders than they can for themselves.

GLOSSARY

AMORTIZATION: Writing off a debt over time.

ARBITRAGE: Taking advantage of differences between one price and another for the same security or commodity.

BERKSHIRE HATHAWAY: Textile company bought by Buffett in 1965 and transformed by him into a hugely successful vehicle for other interests.

BLUE CHIP STAMPS: Trading stamps company bought by Berkshire Hathaway in 1983.

BOOK VALUE: The value placed on a company's assets in the accounts.

BUFFALO EVENING NEWS: Newspaper business purchased by Berkshire Hathaway in 1977.

COLUMBIA GRADUATE BUSINESS SCHOOL: Where Buffett studied for his master's degree and met Benjamin Graham.

DAIRY QUEEN: Chain of ice-cream parlors bought by Berkshire Hathaway in 1997.

ECONOMIC GOODWILL: The value of the earnings of a business over and above its book value.

EXECUTIVE JET AVIATION: Airline business bought by Berkshire Hathaway in 1998.

FINANCIAL GOODWILL: The difference between the higher price paid for a company and the book value of its assets.

FISHER, PHILIP: Famous American investment adviser.

FOCUS INVESTMENT: The concentration of an investor's holdings in a portfolio of only a few stocks.

GENERAL RE: Re-insurance company bought by Berkshire Hathaway in 1998.

GOODWILL ACCOUNTING: *see* Economic goodwill; Financial goodwill.

GRAHAM, BENJAMIN: Investment guru who taught Buffett at Columbia Graduate Business School.

GRAHAM-NEWMAN CORPORATION: Benjamin Graham's investment company in New York, where Buffett worked as a securities analyst.

INTRINSIC BUSINESS VALUE: The true worth of a business, estimated by forecasting future cash inflows and working out their present value.

LOOK-THROUGH EARNINGS: All the underlying profits in which the investor has an ownership.

MARGIN OF SAFETY: The difference between the purchase price of a company's stock and its higher intrinsic value, as advocated by Benjamin Graham and adopted by Buffett.

NEBRASKA FURNITURE MART: Discount furniture business owned by the Blumkin family and bought by Berkshire Hathaway in 1983.

OMAHA, NEBRASKA: Buffett's birthplace and home of Berkshire Hathaway.

OWNER'S MANUAL: 13 owner-related business principles laid down by Buffett primarily for Berkshire Hathaway, but which can be applied to businesses in general.

SCOTT FETZER: Conglomerate owned by Berkshire Hathaway

SEE'S CANDY STORES: Chain of confectionery stores purchased by Berkshire Hathaway in 1972.

STOCK OPTION: The right given to a company employee at an agreed date in the future to buy stock in that company at a price fixed (usually at the then current market level) when the option is awarded.

UNIVERSITY OF NEBRASKA: Where Buffett earned his economics degree.

WHARTON SCHOOL OF FINANCE: Business school in Pennsylvania, attended by Buffett.

BIBLIOGRAPHY

Warren Buffett has never written a book himself, but the gap has been filled to some extent by books drawing on his wit and wisdom. Compilations include *Thoughts of Chairman Buffett* by Simon Reynolds (1998, Harperbusiness, New York), *Warren Buffett Speaks* by Janet C. Lowe (1997, John Wiley & Sons, New York), and Lawrence A. Cunningham's *The Essays of Warren Buffett*; the latter consists of passages selected from the annual reports of Berkshire Hathaway, and these chairman's letters are the best guide to Buffett's thinking.

The fullest account of Buffett's investment philosophy is contained in two books by Robert G. Hagstrom. The first, *The Warren Buffett Way* (1994, John Wiley & Sons, New York), investigates the principles applied by Buffett in selecting and buying stocks. The second, *The Warren Buffett Portfolio*, covering much the same ground, concentrates more on how to manage the stocks profitably after purchase.

Mary Buffett and David Clark wrote *Buffettology* (1997, Scribner, New York) to explain its hero's "previously unexplained techniques." As his former daughter-in-law, Mary Buffett had a privileged view of the great investor at work. There is also *Buffett Step by Step* (1999, Financial Times Management, London), written by Richard Simmons, and rated less highly than the above books. As for the man himself, Andrew Kilpatrick relates his life in *Of Permanent Value* (1994, Andy Kilpatrick Publishing Empire, Birmingham, Alabama), while Roger Lowenstein has contributed *Buffett: The Making of an American Capitalist* (1995, Random House, New York).

Books that have inspired Buffett himself include *Developing an Investment Philosophy* (1991, Pacific Publishing Group, USA) by Philip A. Fisher, and *The Intelligent Investor* by Benjamin Graham. Buffett provided the foreword for the fourth edition of Graham's seminal work.

WORKS CITED

Berkshire Hathaway Annual Reports.

Lawrence A. Cunningham (1997) *The Essays of Warren Buffett: Lessons for Corporate America* (The Cunningham Group, USA).

Benjamin Graham (1985) *The Intelligent Investor: A Book of Practical Counsel* (HarperCollins, New York).

Robert G. Hagstrom (1999) *The Warren Buffett Portfolio: Mastering the Power of the Focus Investment Strategy* (John Wiley & Sons, New York).

Index

INDEX

Robert Heller

Robert Heller is himself a prolific author of management books. The first, *The Naked Manager*, published in 1972, established Heller as an iconoclastic, wide-ranging guide to managerial excellence – and incompetence. Heller has drawn on the extensive knowledge of managers and management he acquired as the founding editor of *Management Today*, Britain's premier business magazine, which he headed for 25 years. Books such as *The Supermanagers*, *The Decision-makers*, *The Superchiefs* and (most recently), *In Search of European Excellence* have all emphasized how to succeed by using the latest ideas on change, quality, and motivation. In 1990 Heller wrote *Culture Shock*, one of the first books to describe how information technology would revolutionize management and business. Since then, as writer, lecturer, and consultant, Heller has continued to tell managers how to "Ride the Revolution." His books for Dorling Kindersley's Essential Managers series are international bestsellers.